A SHORT TREATISE ON ETHICS

A SHORT TREATISE
ON ETHICS

Felix Grayeff

Duckworth

First published in 1980 by
Gerald Duckworth & Company Limited
The Old Piano Factory, 43 Gloucester Crescent, London N.W.1

© 1980 by Felix Grayeff

ISBN 0 7156 1494 0

British Library Cataloguing in Publication Data

Grayeff, Felix
    A short treatise on ethics.
    1. Ethics
    I. Title
    170   BJ1012
    ISBN 0-7156-1494-0

Printed in Great Britain by
Ebenezer Baylis and Son Limited
The Trinity Press, Worcester, and London

Contents

PART ONE: Historical Survey of Ethics

PART TWO: Outline of a Theory of Ethics

PART ONE
Historical Survey of Ethics

Introduction ✓

The following three observations about morals will, I hope, meet with a large measure of approval: (1) that moral perfection has never been achieved; (2) that the moral standards in fully developed, civilized countries are higher than those which obtain, or have obtained, in primitive or less fully developed regions; (3) that the gap between perfection and the morals in civilized countries is immeasurably wider than the gap which divides the standards in civilized countries from those in primitive parts. From these observations the following conclusions can be drawn: that whereas moral perfection remains far off, some moral progress, though by no means steady progress, is capable of being brought about; and since some progress has been made in the past it should be possible for further progress to be achieved in the future.

Ethical problems have received attention since early times and ethical doctrines, or even systems of ethics, have been propounded by many eminent thinkers for centuries past. It is therefore hardly possible for a modern philosopher to discuss moral problems without giving full consideration to the history of ethics. For not only are we all influenced by past thought, even if we are unaware of it, but it is almost inconceivable to say anything worthwhile or valid on ethics without deliberately drawing on the reflections of previous thinkers. Therefore we must begin our ethical studies by offering a historical survey, however brief, of moral philosophy from ancient times to the present.

We distinguish the following nine types of moral theory:

(1) Ethics of perfect virtue or saintliness;
(2) Ethics of achievable virtue;
(3) Ethics of rational selfishness, leading to Utilitarianism;
(4) Naturalistic ethics;
(5) Ethical formalism;
(6) Material or value ethics;

(7) Intuitive ethics;
(8) Relativistic ethics;
(9) Moral scepticism.

Although by its very nature ethics is concerned with conduct, or the behaviour of people towards one another, ethical theory has from the beginning been marked by its tendency to direct attention to the individual by himself rather than as the fellow of other individuals, that is, to the qualities or virtues of the person rather than to his conduct towards other persons.

How is this to be explained? In the first place, through a historical accident, namely, the emphasis placed in early Greek society and in particular aristocratic society on virtue, *aretê*, as the goal of true Hellenic education, however varied the meanings of this word were. In its early stages *aretê* signified not only decency and goodness but also valour, courtly manners and chivalry. Then it came to mean ability, craftsmanship, competence, and only through the impact of philosophy did it acquire the meaning of moral virtue and finally of perfect moral virtue. At the same time, or even earlier, saintliness, that is, perfect virtue in the religious sense or the desire to be as close as possible to the righteous Deity, was extolled in eastern countries.

A. The Greeks

1. The three Aristotelian works on ethics[1] constitute an extraordinary amalgam of (1) a biologically conceived ethics, (2) an ethics concerned with political and sociological problems and (3) an ethics of pure contemplation derived probably from Plato (*Timaeus*) or even from eastern religious thought. Of these three components of Peripatetic thinking on ethics the first has received most attention. This is not only because this part of the Aristotelian ethics contains the famous conception of the 'mean', but also a result of Aristotle's deeply discerning understanding of human motives and human emotions, which are in evidence here.[2] Virtue

---

[1] *Nichomachean Ethics, Eudemian Ethics* and *Magna Moralia*.

[2] See Stuart Hampshire's lucid exposition of the Aristotelian Ethics in *Two Theories of Morality*, Oxford 1977, esp. p. 54.

according to this section of the Aristotelian ethics consists in avoiding extremes, in moderation, in attaining the right and proper mean between excess and deficiency. Take two examples: Man should be courageous, for courage is the mean, or the middle, between cowardice and foolhardiness. Man should be generous: generosity is the mean between miserliness and prodigality.

The conception of the mean has for long been recognized as of biological, or medical, origin. As good health consists in the right state of the body, with its various components in the right balance, so the mind enjoys good health so long as it maintains the right and proper mean, that is, so long as all its qualities avoid excess on the one side and deficiency on the other.

Through this conception of the mean, although it refers to virtue rather than to conduct, the Aristotelian ethics is linked to the true needs of man or the realities of life, and therefore may be classified as an ethics of achievable virtue. Nevertheless, in another part of his work on morals, Aristotle also refers to and extols the virtue of pure contemplation, viz. of the heavenly bodies in their majestic and harmonious movements.[1] The exercise of this virtue, Aristotle says, flows from the worthiest part of human nature, the intellect or mind, because the intellect (*nous*) contemplates the heavens and is therefore sometimes called by Aristotle the divine element in man. However, let it be emphasized at this point that, according to Aristotle, the divine in man, that is, the intellect, is only the worthiest or highest of the components which make up human nature and is not separated from the remaining constituents of man.

Now, according to Greek thinking, as we shall presently explain, the exercise of the highest virtue is necessarily accompanied by the greatest happiness man can possibly find—a happiness equal to that of the gods, as Aristotle says. It is clear therefore that, whereas Aristotle's ethics of the mean, or moderation, represents a philosophy of attainable virtue, his ethics of contemplation belongs rather to another category of ethics, that of perfect virtue necessarily followed by the greatest happiness, or beatitude.[2] It is difficult to deny that these two types of ethics as well as the third,

[1] On the best life, cf. *Nichomachean Ethics* 15; VII, 12; X 7; *Eudemian Ethics* I, 5, VIII, 3. See also *Metaphysics* XII, 7.

[2] Traces of Aristotle's politically oriented ethics are found in *Nichomachean Ethics* I, 1f., x, and in the *Eudemian Ethics*.

the politically related ethics to which we alluded before,[1] are markedly different classes of moral philosophy. The ethics of the mean derives from the scientific strain in the Peripatetic school, whereas the philosophy of pure contemplation goes back to Plato and, as mentioned, possibly to oriental religious influences.

2. Socrates was the first to place moral questions in the centre of philosophical debate. He and Plato after him inquired: What is valour, justice, piety, virtue? Yet it was left to the early Stoa not only to make of ethics the apex of a philosophical system but also to form a conception of perfect virtue which has never been surpassed, at least not as far as secular philosophy is concerned. Its essence is that only he who consistently and fully and in all his doings acts in accordance with the spirit (*logos*) which permeates nature and gives nature its eternal rule, and which is sometimes called 'God' in Stoic literature, is virtuous, is a 'sage' (*sophos*). It follows that the virtuous do not act in compliance with the laws and customs of men but in accordance with nature, which is ruled by reason. And since reason is stronger than passions—love, hate, sorrow, pity—the sage will overcome in himself all that might divert him from the path of virtue and in particular his passions.

To the Stoic mind virtue is all; it is self-sufficient. It is a higher goal than health, riches or power. Conversely, nothing short of perfect virtue is adequate. Nor can anything else make an individual happy. Indeed, according to Stoic thinking, the poor and virtuous are far happier than those who are rich and powerful but lack virtue.

Like the word virtue, so the word happiness underwent a long process of evolution. The Greek for 'happy' is '*eudaimôn*' which, literally translated, means 'favoured by the gods'. In early usage the happy man was the one who enjoyed great power and was allowed by the gods to have his desires and aspirations fulfilled. Then, under the influence of philosophical analysis, the word happiness acquired the meaning of contentedness or satisfaction with one's own lot. Finally in Stoic usage it came to mean that inner peace which results from the possession of perfect virtue and which implies freedom from all disturbing passions: serenity.

Correspondingly, the meaning of the word 'good' (*to agathon*) was altered: to the naive mind and to the Sophists it meant

[1] See my *Aristotle and his School*, London 1974, pp. 164–6.

pleasure, albeit sometimes in a refined sense, but to the philosophers and especially the Stoics it signified full virtue, or rather happiness obtained through virtue.

Originally the Stoics taught that nothing short of perfect virtue should be the aim of all men, but later, during the epochs of the middle Stoa and the late Stoa, the Stoic philosophers also allowed for lesser virtue; in other words, they decided on a grading of virtues. The possession of full virtue remained the ultimate objective, for which the Stoic term was *katorthôma*; their term for the lesser virtues was *ta kathêkonta*, which meant all that was decent or fair or a matter of duty. These duties, the Stoics held, should be fulfilled even by those who did not possess perfect virtue, that is, by ordinary people who did not reach the height of wisdom in the full sense of the word and therefore could not be called 'sages'. Nor could the fulfilment of these lesser duties ever amount to the attainment of absolute virtue. It consisted in obeying precepts such as 'Honour your parents', 'Help your friends', 'Serve your country'.

The religious term for perfect happiness is beatitude, and not surprisingly it is possible to find close parallels between the Stoic philosophy and the teachings of the Bible. There are even grounds justifying the view that the Stoa derived its original inspiration from biblical ethics.[1] For, as the pupils of the Stoics endeavoured to act in harmony with the *logos* which permeates nature, so a saintly person tries to be as close to the Deity as he can, or even to emulate God in his justice, righteousness, grace and self-sacrificing mercy. (These last two attributes of the Christian God are, however, absent from Stoic thinking.)

Any ethics of perfection, like the one for which the Stoics are famous, contains great risks. It has often been argued that a lofty idea or goal, even though the goal itself may remain beyond anyone's reach, spurs people to ever more strenuous attempts to attain the ideal. This may be true in some remarkable or unusual cases, but since all moral theory ought to be adapted to the needs of ordinary men and women it is right to say that the setting up of a goal so sublime that it can never be achieved, far from encouraging people to reach out for ever greater heights, leads, on the contrary, to ethical scepticism, cynicism and indeed hypocrisy—in a religious context the kind of hypocrisy which is displayed by Molière's Tartuffe and by which his Orgon is deceived.

[1] Cf. *Arnim*, s.v., F.III, pp. 134f.

No category of ethics has made a deeper impact on moral thought and the ethical standards of many people than the ethics of perfection. But for this very reason it has also caused much confusion. For, by placing before men and women, and especially the young, an ideal of moral conduct which it is palpably impossible ever to realize, it has on the one hand, led to contempt of such ethical behaviour as it is feasible for men to live up to, and, on the other, induced individuals to masquerade as having—almost—attained perfection of conduct. In short it has made hypocrisy a common feature of human life or interhuman relations. Moreover, such hypocrisy is frequently accompanied by harshness, disguised as a demand for the highest standards and the highest only, by self-righteousness and inflexibility displayed both in the smallest circles—of family and friends—and in public. The early Stoics, mentioned above as the champions of the secular ethics of perfection, condemned as absolutely guilty all those who did not possess absolute virtue: and thus, almost uniquely among philosophers, they went so far as to make pity an immoral emotion. Show no pity to the suffering, they taught, because all suffering, all unhappiness, is self-induced: caused either by over-indulgence in food, drink and so on, or simply by a person's unwillingness to rise above his unhappiness. Analogously, religion teaches people to judge themselves severely: to inflict physical and psychological punishment on themselves, to atone for sins perhaps never committed, to abandon themselves to the torments of a guilty conscience, to expect the most terrifying retribution in after-life, even though they may formally disbelieve in the certainty of such retribution.

And beyond that, many false liberals in our own time, while shutting their eyes to the injustices taking place around them, scan the horizon of the inhabited world and on the pretence of perfection condemn injustices—undeniably real and reprehensible—in far-away countries, but do it on a selective basis, whether or not deliberately, and often go so far as to recommend merciless methods of punishment to avenge the injustices they have chosen to condemn.

3. In sharp contrast to philosophical, and in particular Stoic, teaching, the Sophists conceived of the good, of happiness and of *aretê* in a manner far closer to the views of the common people, but, like the Stoics, they went to extremes in expressing their views. In

its crudest form the Sophists' view, which can be expressed as the simple formula 'Right is might', is stated by Thrasymachus in the first book of Plato's *Republic*. In a more sophisticated way, and indeed in a manner acceptable even to many people today, the Sophists' view is made clear by Protagoras (in Plato's *Theaetetus* 167c), who says: 'Whatever is thought just and admirable in any city is regarded as just and admirable by the citizens of that city for so long as it is thought just and admirable in that city.'

It is easy to recognize in this statement an early intimation of a type of ethics which has received much attention in our time, namely by those engaged in the study of society, the sociologists. Still, in its own time it was rejected as an ethical doctrine under the weight of Plato's arguments; and neither in classical antiquity nor since have Protagoras and the Sophists been regarded as moral philosophers, for the simple reason that they seem to deny the validity of any objective rules of conduct. They seem to teach that all is allowed to him who has the power to do all.

4. However, yet another Greek philosophical school, which championed many views similar to those of the Sophists, not only had many followers in the Graeco-Roman period but has remained influential to some extent even in modern times—the school of Epicurus. Of course, Epicurus' views have always been highly controversial: though they were accepted by some philosophers as the basis of their own thought, they have more frequently been chosen as the target of moral criticism and indeed invective, mainly on account of Epicurus' supposedly wholly materialistic approach to the problems not only of epistemology but of ethics.

The principal point at issue is the significance accorded to the concept of happiness, which Epicurus defines in a twofold way: as pleasure resulting from the fulfilment of one's desires, and as the absence of, or the opposite of pleasure—namely, pain. The Greek word for pleasure is *hêdonê* and hence the Epicurean type of ethics has become known as *hedonism*. Now certain philosophers, including Kant, have considered the desire for happiness not only as an impulse irrelevant to moral philosophy but as the very opposite of that force within or above us which makes us act morally; and they have consequently endeavoured to exclude hedonism or Epicureanism from moral philosophy altogether, on the grounds that Epicurus —even if he recognizes moral values—accepts them not *per se* but only as a means to an end, as being conducive to pleasure. That of course is true as far as it goes, and it is also true to say that Epicurus makes self-interest the mainspring of human action. However, in doing so he does not deviate essentially from other Greek philosophers: to the Greek mind self-interest and virtue leading to happiness were not opposites, as they seem to have become in modern times. Indeed there are aspects of Epicurus' philosophy which make it a true ethics: Epicurus links pleasure to such virtues as self-restraint, fortitude, righteousness and so on, because, he says, pleasure cannot be attained by those who do not control themselves or their appetites and are plagued by the fear of death and the dread of vengeful gods. Moreover Epicurus grades the different kinds of pleasure, assessing their relative values and stressing good sense—*phronêsis*—as an indispensable requirement by which the proper priorities of the various virtues leading to pleasure are established. Thus he teaches that thought is the prerequisite to reaching the highest goal, happiness. Moreover since, like the Stoics, he regards passions as disturbances and compares them with tempests (as Democritus had before him), he calls on his followers to master their passions by controlling them through the exercise of reason, until at last they enjoy the state of *ataraxia*, imperturbability.[1]

It follows that the philosophy of Epicurus by no means amounts to a negation of ethics but is a possible form of it.

B. The Renaissance

We have found that many, though by no means all, aspects of moral philosophy as we know it were present in the ethics of the ancient world. It is equally apparent that most of the great antitheses which have marked moral philosophy till today are already found in antiquity. They are as follows:

---

[1] The followers of Epicurus sometimes lived together in happy communities; see A. J. Festugière, *Epicurus and his Gods*, Oxford 1955. But what made their happy communal life possible was each individual's own well-tempered soul and disposition.

(1) An ethics of universal validity as against an ethics of changing conventions;
(2) An ethics seeking moral perfection as against an ethics seeking achievable virtue;
(3) An ethics of reason attempting to overcome passion, as against a theory of unrestricted self-interest or enjoyment of pleasure;
(4) An ethics primarily of virtue or self-improvement, as against an ethics relating primarily to conduct;
(5) An ethics concerned with the life of the private individual only, as against an ethics indissolubly linked to politics.

On the other hand, the following contrasts which were hardly evident in the Graeco-Roman period have proved significant since then:

(1) An ethics of universal reason, as against forms of ethics based on individuals' propensities;
(2) A formalistic ethics, as against a 'material ethics', i.e. an ethics of values.

Although the influence of classical thinking on modern philosophy, including ethics, has been strong and permanent, yet modern ethics derived its immediate impulse not from classical philosophy but from medieval, Christian, thinking. It did so in a twofold, contradictory, way. Modern ethics is characterized on the one hand by its inability to shake off the impact of medieval ethics and on the other by its reaction against it and its resolution to free itself from it completely. Therefore, before we can turn to a discussion of modern ethics, we must give some attention to the new moral concepts which appeared during the Middle Ages. First of all, certain new virtues, of which the ancient thinkers and Graeco-Roman society in general knew nothing, emerged and still feature prominently in the moral code of the Church—namely, humility, obedience, resistance to the desires of the flesh, in short self-denial and self-sacrifice. Thus Christian ethics directly or indirectly introduced into moral philosophy a distinction between selfishness and unselfishness—the first associated with the flesh, the second with the soul—which was alien to the ancient world. For such qualities as obedience or the readiness to sacrifice oneself were not considered virtues by the ancient philosophers, at least not in the sense that they should be practised for their own sake, though self-denial or self-sacrifice for one's own country or even for a friend may have been subsidiary virtues in the eyes of the Greek thinkers—namely, in relation to other virtues such as courage or generosity.

When therefore, during and after the Renaissance, ethical philosophers attempted to liberate themselves from the teaching of the medieval Church, some were unable to free their views completely from the influence of religious morality. Hence they developed ethical theories which, unlike Greek moral doctrines, were—and have remained—characterized by a growing intensification of the contrast between an ethics striving for pure virtue and one strictly derived from self-interest. Just as certain medieval virtues had no place in Greek thought, so this antithesis between selfishness and unselfishness had no place in it either, at least not in the sense they are known to us in the modern era. On the contrary, 'the good', *aretê* (virtue) and happiness were commonly accepted as the ultimate aims of all human actions, even though the various philosophical schools put different interpretations on these three key notions of their ethical thinking and accordingly devised different ways by which to attain these aims. Still, even the Stoics, who made absolute virtue the one condition of true happiness, agreed that the primary impulse of every creature was self-protection; while the Epicureans, on the other hand, though they regarded happiness as the ultimate goal, called for sound sense and self-restraint in the pursuit of it.

After so many centuries of religious teaching which stressed above all the cleavage between soul and body, between the divine and the earthly (profane) in man, all subsequent philosophical schools started either from the higher side of man's nature—the idealist schools—or from the material condition of human life—the so-called materialist or sociological schools. Be it added, however, that few philosophers followed one or the other of those extremes exclusively. On the contrary, most of them tried to achieve some kind of synthesis, even though one or the other of the opposing viewpoints would be dominant in any particular school or at any rate was ascribed to it by the historians. Moreover ethical scepticism, usually allied to materialism, began to play an increasing part.

1. Of the Renaissance philosophers whose aim it was to break away from the moral philosophy of the Church and to base their own ethics not on revelation but on scientific enquiry, Thomas Hobbes is perhaps the most eminent. The object of science is to explore nature, and hence it was from nature that Hobbes attempted to derive his ethico-political theory. Since ethics is concerned with man, Hobbes investigated *human* nature and found that its essence, or main motivating force, was the impulse to self-preservation. This led him to a second and equally significant conclusion, namely, that as man lives among his fellow-men his impulse towards self-preservation is exercised in his struggle not merely with nature but also with his fellow-men. And by approaching the problems of ethics from this new starting-point, Hobbes changed ethics from a theory mainly, or centrally, concerned with the improvement of self, or the achievement of virtue, to a philosophy of conduct.

Hobbes remains admirable both for his realism and his unity of thought. As he made selfishness the sole motive of human action, he consistently taught that such conduct as is usually called moral must flow also from self-interest. Hobbes's doctrines are too well-known to require more than the briefest recapitulation. It is best to start from his conception of the origin of the state, which he regards as an association of the inhabitants of a region formed for the purpose of their mutual self-protection. For Hobbes believed that in primordial times everybody had to fight everybody else for food, shelter, self-preservation. Those primitive conditions he called *bellum omnium contra omnes*. Now, to escape from the unbearable hardships of such a state of affairs, people decided to appoint one from their midst as their superior—their sovereign; and they gave this appointed sovereign the task of protecting all individuals from injury or—which is the same—of preventing any particular individual from injuring his fellow-men. To make this new, orderly, state of things stable and permanent—Hobbes explains—the people concluded a contract with their sovereign, binding him to the fulfilment of his task and themselves to obey him. This contract, they decided, was to be inviolable because, if it were not, the old chaos of perpetual warfare would inevitably return.

Since the sovereign was to carry out his task by issuing laws and enforcing them, and since those laws were designed to protect individuals from the wrongs other individuals might wish to inflict on them, a man who lived in a community under an enforceable law would act against his own interest if ever he openly broke the law, because if he did he would lay himself open to punishment. It further followed that such protection as the law or the state afforded was in the interest of all; and hence that a state of lawfulness naturally flowed from self-interest. All citizens or subjects of a sovereign stood to gain from the laws, or from the rules of conduct imposed by the state on each of them.

It is easy to appreciate that the link between ethics and politics has never before been so close as in the philosophy of Hobbes.[1] Later, Hobbes's successors in the nineteenth century, the Utilitarians, strengthened this link still further: there can be no ethical or considerate behaviour, they held, except through the state or, as they preferred to call it, society. In the view of the Utilitarians the state was created to satisfy the need, or desire, for considerate conduct.

One of Hobbes's conclusions deserves special mention: his understanding of the essence of power. The concept of power belongs to the modern period. The Greeks had not formed it; it was created during the Renaissance. That great realist Macchiavelli introduced it to the general consciousness of philosophers, and Bacon took it up in the context of his philosophy of science. Bacon thought that the ultimate purpose of scientific enquiry was in fact power—not only power over nature, but power over one's own, less knowledgeable, fellow-men. Hobbes, however, who of course had read Bacon with keen attention, was the earliest philosopher to see (and I do not know if this has ever been fully appreciated) that power is immaterial. It may appear strange that power should not be material in every sense, as one is normally inclined to believe. But this is what Hobbes discovered. 'Reputation of power *is* power; because it draweth with it the adherence of those that need protection'.[2] That Hobbes is right in this will be clear from the following reflection. Although a sovereign of course commands a large army of soldiers and a great number of civil servants and through them, because they enforce his will, possesses power, he is

[1] Whereas according to Greek thought the state exists to enable each of its citizens to develop his own virtue to the fullest, Hobbes held that the state was created to make it possible for a balance to be struck and maintained between the conflicting selfish wishes of the individual and the interest of all.

[2] *Leviathan*, ch. x, p. 41 of the original edition.

powerful only as long as his authority is recognized and his will obeyed. No one will doubt that it is difficult for people to shake off their habitual, general readiness to submit to an established governing authority. But regimes have been overthrown, and will be overthrown, each time by a similar process, namely—and here we return to Hobbes—the formation of new groupings acquiring a reputation, and thereby authority.

Equally, it is of great interest to see how Hobbes explains why men strive for power. The desire to obtain power and then increase it perpetually, he says, stems from the need for security; because, to safeguard oneself, a pre-emptive attack is the best and most natural way of self-defence. For an individual's attempt to protect himself is endangered as soon as some other individual attains greater power than he has gained himself. Hence he must forever seek an increase in his own strength so that he is not deprived of the strength he already possesses. 'Man cannot be content with a moderate power because he cannot assure the power and means to live well which he hath present, without the acquisition of more. And from hence kings whose power is greatest turn their endeavours to the assuring it at home by laws or abroad by wars'.[1] This explanation is indispensable for an understanding of the incredible mistakes made by such great conquerors as Charles XII of Sweden, Napoleon and others.

Hobbes has been called a 'materialist' because, in the first place, he believes that all human emotions, representations, thought and so on are of a physical nature, or rather reflexes of bodily changes; and secondly because he roots his theory firmly in experience only and thereby excludes any transcendent or metaphysical source of moral behaviour, or of the moral command, in contrast to later philosophers, especially Kant. He has also been described as a 'naturalist', since his experience is gathered from observations of nature. Generally, as explained before, enquiry into nature was the Renaissance philosophers' response, or alternative, to the Church's demand that revelation should be accepted unquestioningly as the only source of knowledge; and Hobbes's reaction to Church dogma, and especially to the schoolmen's division of human nature into an animal and a divine element, was so vehement that it led him to exclude from his philosophy the divine constituent altogether and

[1] Ibid., ch. XI, p. 47.

derive his ethics solely from man's earthly nature.[1] His objective was to show that man's animal or wordly nature was sufficient to explain considerate or ethical conduct; and it is in this aspect of his work that his claim to be one of the great moral philosophers lies.[2]

2. Hobbes was preceded, and no doubt influenced, by another thinker who made nature his guide, a jurist rather than a philosopher, Hugo Grotius. Grotius remains memorable because he was the first to conceive the idea of imposing restrictions even on the way in which nations fight wars. He thereby became the founder of the law of nations—international law—and his influence has been powerfully felt ever since the publication of his *De Iure Belli et Pacis* in 1625. The Geneva Convention, limiting or barring the use of certain weapons in war, or making the care of the wounded or prisoners of war obligatory at least for all those governments which have signed the Convention, is the continuing effect of Grotius' work. Before Grotius it was generally assumed that in war everything was permitted. No horror, cruelty or infamy was banned, because even the worst actions could be excused on the grounds that they were a means to a legitimate end, namely, victory over the enemy. 'Deceit, cruelty, injustice are the proper business of battles' (Tertullian). As against this, Grotius taught as a general principle that certain humane or humanizing laws or precepts applied even to the conduct of war, and he proceeded to formulate such laws in detail. Though we are not concerned with any of Grotius' special rules, it will be useful to give at least one example. That it is legitimate, when a beleaguered city refuses to surrender, for the besiegers to threaten the men in the city with death but not the women with rape, is one of Grotius' international laws.

Like Hobbes, Grotius derived his rules from nature, although, unlike Hobbes, he also appealed to divine law. What makes his

---

[1] Although Bishop Butler (1692–1752) opposes the doctrines of Hobbes and his successors and insists that revelation must remain the prime guide for our actions, he is, nevertheless, influenced by the 'new learning' and attempts to incorporate it in his teaching as a whole. While he considers that the moral laws are given to us by God he yet emphasizes that our motive to obey them stems from our dual desire to be judged good both by God and by our fellow-men.

[2] In our own century Hobbes, together with the Stoics, Spinoza, Hume and even Kant, has been accused (by G. E. Moore and Moore's followers) of having committed the 'naturalistic fallacy'. For an explanation of this accusation and whether or not it is justified, see below, pp. 47ff.

work so important, however, in an ethical context is not so much the way in which he derives his theory as the fact that a jurist-philosopher tried to prove—indeed did successfully prove—the necessity and validity of moral rules in all circumstances.

3. Spinoza like Hobbes, based his ethical views on nature but, unlike Hobbes, not merely on human nature but on nature as a whole. Further, again in conformity with other Renaissance philosophers, he understood by nature not what the Church meant by it but the cosmos as penetrable to science, that is, to the human mind. However, the doctrine which distinguishes him from other thinkers is his conclusion that nature is subjected to unchangeable, necessary rules. He conceived of the cosmos as one great unity dominated by, and functioning through, its own physico-mathematical, causal, necessary laws.

Now, considering the condition of man within nature, Spinoza like Hobbes traced all human actions back to man's impulses or desires for self-preservation and the acquisition of the means of life; and rejecting all dogmatic conceptions of 'good' and 'evil', he—like Hobbes—regarded as bad whatever hinders us and as good whatever is helpful and useful to us.

Although this doctrine applies generally both to external circumstances and to man's internal condition, Spinoza's emphasis falls on the latter. He discusses in detail man's passions—anger, hatred, envy—and he believes that these passions are the main impediments to the kind of life which is desirable for us or, indeed, which is desired by us. Moreover he succeeds in reducing all our passions to one (twin) source, namely, the desire for pleasure and flight from pain. In this he surpasses at any rate his immediate predecessors, who had described the various passions but had not tried to find their root-cause.[1] One further aspect of his teaching stands out. Spinoza stresses the need for absolute truthfulness towards oneself and others. He sets out with determination to tear away the veils of self-deception because, as he says, it is every man's natural right to exercise, and as far as possible implement, his impulse to self-preservation. Hence everybody is justified in admitting that he is selfish in this sense.

We come now to what is unique in Spinoza's philosophy and

[1] At this point Spinoza incorporates one of Epicurus' theories in his own philosophy.

distinguishes him from all his predecessors and indeed successors. Many commentators have been puzzled by the choice of title, *Ethica*, for his main work, which contains his philosophical system in its entirety. On the face of it, his philosophy is a theistic metaphysics rather than an ethics. Yet Spinoza considered the ethical part of his work as its most important aspect, and rightly so because ultimately he aimed at deriving the rules of ethics from nature as he saw it, that is, from nature as dominated by the laws of absolute necessity. How could he possibly arrive at this conclusion? He did so by uniting the attainment of virtue to the basic motive of self-interest, that is, by uniting freedom and necessity or, in technical terms, the doctrines of free will and determinism. We act as we choose, Spinoza says, but we *must* choose what is good for us, and it is good for us to purge ourselves of our passions, because to be freed of our passions is tantamount to achieving happiness and also to being virtuous.[1] In this way Spinoza makes virtue flow from self-interest, from necessity.[2]

The second pivotal concept of Spinoza's ethics is power. In this he follows Bacon rather than Hobbes, because he sees power mainly as wisdom. Wisdom is power in the sense that it entails an understanding of nature and its necessary laws, thereby making it possible for man to serve his own supreme interest. Moreover Spinoza's concept of wisdom also comprises shrewdness. Every individual, according to Spinoza, aims at living in peace and tranquillity in the company of his fellow-men; but, unless you can make your fellows understand what God and nature are, you cannot achieve your aim, which is peace. Therefore all other people's knowledge of nature is as beneficial to you as your own knowledge is beneficial to everyone else.

And so, by exercising wisdom, which is power, man not only follows nature, or shows himself to be part of it, but mirrors all nature in himself—in his own being and his actions. And since nature and God are one and the same, the ultimate aim of man is to recreate the Deity in himself, that is, in humanity. In other words,

---

[1] Freedom, which is freedom from passions, is a necessity, because to be free from passion is to be happy and we necessarily desire to be happy. We call freedom from passions virtue, not because we *want* to be free of passions but because it is in our natural interest to be free in this sense.

[2] This is true of man in general, but of course Spinoza admits that there are persons who are unable to free themselves of the 'bondage of their passions'.

it is man's function to emulate the Deity, to make *imitatio Dei*, his supreme objective.

Of all ethical philosophers Spinoza alone teaches that we *must* aim at virtue and *must* be good. In Spinoza's ethics there is no 'Thou shalt' but only a 'Thou art'—that is to say, you, or we, are seeking self-improvement, compelled to do so by nature, or nature's laws, which are the divine laws. For to follow our basic impulse, namely of self-preservation, we must act both wisely and shrewdly, thereby realizing what is good for us and acquiring the various virtues. One may speak of an implicit determinism in Spinoza's philosophy, but it is a determinism quite different from the later materialistic or psychological version of this theory. For, according to Spinoza, although the will is not free, it is directed towards one goal, and that goal is to emulate God who is free. For God, being pure intelligence, does not know the 'tempests' of the passions; he is independent of that which holds man in bondage—man's craving for pleasure and fear of pain.

To sum up, Spinoza stands out among philosophers in that he binds together two utter extremes: perfect virtue and absolute selfishness. That is to say, only Spinoza succeeds in deriving the highest virtue from the most common, most human impulse—that of seeking what is most desirable for oneself. Equally he succeeds to a higher degree than any other philosopher in evolving his entire ethical philosophy from one root, the necessity of man's selfishness; and whereas Hobbes speaks of several laws of nature, Spinoza reduces all rules to one, the law of necessity as it applies equally to man, nature and the Deity.

But of course, despite his almost unequalled originality, Spinoza also depends on his predecessors in several respects. His ethics is an ethics of the soul, rather than of conduct, like the moral theories of the Greek philosophers—Aristotle and even more markedly the early Stoics. Spinoza follows Aristotle in making the contemplation of the Deity and the cosmos the cause of the greatest happiness, and so considers it the supreme virtue. He was influenced by the Stoic concept of the *logos*, which permeates nature, and which he transformed into divine necessity functioning within nature, *Deus sive Natura*. Further, he was obviously inspired by the Stoic precept that man should live in accordance with nature.[1] For in his

---

[1] Spinoza expressly states that because happiness flows from virtue we consider virtue as good and vice as evil (*Ethica*, pt. IV, prop. XVIII). Thus Spinoza

view, too, happiness is dependent on virtue and virtue is obtained by those individuals who follow the law of nature.[1]

C. The Eighteenth Century

1. A common bond unites the English, Irish and Scottish philosophers of the seventeenth and eighteenth centuries: all of them followed the model of empirical science in developing their moral doctrines, namely, by basing them on human psychology. The earliest of these ethical thinkers, Cumberland (1632–1719), enjoys the special merit of having taught, in direct contrast to Hobbes and Spinoza, that the ultimate mainspring of all human actions is not self-interest alone but self-interest allied to what he called 'benevolence', that is, our impulse to be kind to others. This was an important step forward, though Cumberland no doubt was influenced by Grotius, according to whose teaching human nature encompasses an *appetitus societatis*, i.e. a man's desire to spend his life in the company of his fellow-men. However, there is this difference between Grotius and Cumberland: in Grotius' view, to be kind to our fellow-beings is part of our selfishness, that is, our selfish *appetitus*, whereas Cumberland was the first—at any rate among modern philosophers or preachers—to conceive of bene-volence as a primary and irreducible property of our nature. In this sense he is the precursor of the greatest of the English or even—as I believe—all moral philosophers, Hume. Yet, either because he was unable to extricate himself from religious ethics or perhaps, on the

---

teaches that we desire what is good, in contrast to philosophers who hold that what is good is determined by our wishes, i.e. that we call good whatever we desire.

[1] The question whether Spinoza was an 'ethical naturalist' has recently been discussed at some length by Paul D. Eisenberg in *Philosophia*, vol. 7, 1 (an issue almost entirely devoted to Spinoza), pp. 107–33. There Eisenberg refers to W. K. Frankena's interpretation of an 'ethical naturalist as a philosopher who attempts to derive ethical conclusions from statements describing facts'. Although this interpretation appears to me more formal (logical) than illuminat-ing, I agree with Eisenberg's conclusion that Spinoza deduces his ethical laws from nature while at the same time basing them on his own metaphysical theistic conception of nature as a whole.

contrary, because he did not venture to depart too far from the 'new learning' as represented by Hobbes, Cumberland viewed selfishness and benevolence as two conflicting tendencies within man's nature and hence held that, as we live our lives, every one of our actions implies a struggle between self-interest and benevolence, and that each time the outcome of this struggle means victory for either the one or the other of our own two primary, natural, inclinations. It is clear that in elaborating this aspect of his philosophy, Cumberland resuscitated the dualism which was so characteristic of Christian medieval morality and which Hobbes and Spinoza seemed to have overcome and replaced, though at a great price—namely, the price of overlooking and ignoring benevolence.

Cumberland's immediate successors, Shaftesbury, Hutchison and Hume, also dwelt on the conflict between good and bad within ourselves, or the struggle between self-interest and benevolence which Cumberland had placed in the forefront of philosophical discussion. These thinkers, however, made it their main task to determine as precisely as they could the essence of that propensity within us, benevolence, which Cumberland had stressed.

Shaftesbury (1671-1713) appears to have been the first among modern philosophers to have seen a basic connection between moral and aesthetic concepts, and by analogy with what he believed to be the truly beautiful he thought that there existed the truly good. Hence he held that, exactly as true beauty was not relative but absolute and permanent and wherever true beauty was manifest it could not but be acknowledged by any healthy mind, so the truly good was autonomous, universal and permanent. It was in this context that Shaftesbury asserted that we were gifted not only with an aesthetic but also with a 'moral sense'—a phrase he coined.

With this doctrine Shaftesbury revived the Greek combination—almost the unity—of the good and the beautiful, that is, the ancient notion of virtue as a beautiful thing to contemplate. We see, then, that it was Greek thinking that produced the shift from Cumberland's theory to those of his immediate successors. Moreover, as has long been recognized, Shaftesbury's notion of the autonomy of the good had a great impact on Kant's moral philosophy, which is based on the doctrine of the autonomy of practical reason.

Although Hutchison (1694-1747), like Shaftesbury, was convinced of a profound connection between virtue and beauty, he differed from Shaftesbury in not reflecting on the object of our moral inclination, namely, the good itself, but concentrated on an analysis of our own faculties of perceiving both the good and the beautiful; and, dividing our innate faculties into (a) intellectual and (b) sensuous properties, he decided that our moral property was sensuous or emotional and not intellectual. (In this, as we shall see, he was followed by Hume but vehemently opposed by Kant.) Hutchison made taste his key-conception; yet, whereas Shaftesbury had merely established an analogy between the beautiful and the good, Hutchison held that, exactly as we perceive that objects are beautiful or ugly, so we perceive that the objects of actions or objectives are good or bad, and that we must approve of the good and must disapprove of the bad. Accordingly, like Shaftesbury, Hutchison considered beauty and virtue absolute and permanent. He explained these two aspects of his aesthetic and ethical doctrines by stating that the moral taste, like the aesthetic taste, was not personal, but general or universal, and that it was subject to necessary laws, that is to say laws valid for all mankind, or at least for all those who do not allow themselves to be swayed by partiality and prejudices or who are perverse by nature.

Both Shaftesbury's and Hutchison's works have had a remarkable influence on later thinking. They have contributed to the view frequently expressed in the nineteenth and twentieth centuries that the values of secular culture are equal or even superior to the values of an education based on religion. Such views, however, were not the doctrines which Hutchison intended to propagate, and it is wrong to hold him responsible for the modern outgrowths of his teaching, or indeed to praise him as one of the great prophets of idealistic philosophy, as Windelband has done.[1] On the other hand, Hutchison's approach to moral philosophy may well be criticized for a different reason, namely, that he by-passes the essential requirements of ethical thinking by concentrating on enquiries into what our moral inclination consists of, or what it can be compared with (namely, aesthetic taste), or even from where it stems. For the main aim and objective of all ethical theory is to discover how a general improvement of conduct can be achieved.

2. As one compares the works of Hume's predecessors with his own, one is easily tempted into concluding that his contribution to ethical theory was rather insignificant. Yet Hume is the leading

[1] Windelband, *History of Philosophy*, vol. 2.

moral philosopher of the seventeenth and early eighteenth centuries, rising above all others not only by the clarity and good sense of his argumentation but also by his humanity. No philosopher has observed the human heart with a closer understanding, or philosophized about the problems of ethics with a deeper feeling or a clearer appreciation of what is right and wrong.

The chief merit of Hume's thought is that it unifies the finest results of the arguments of his predecessors. Hume followed Hobbes in deriving all human action from one source. Like Cumberland, he made benevolence the second of man's two original motives of action, next to self-love, and he insisted with great force as Hutchison had asserted before him, that moral action is prompted not by reason but by sentiment or emotion.

These were the views which Hume succeeded in combining and the synthesis of which under one idea constitutes his own moral doctrine—which, incidentally, he himself regarded as the most valuable part of his entire philosophical work (*An Enquiry concerning the Principles of Morals, 1751*).

The new concept which Hume introduced into moral philosophy is of an emotion he called 'sympathy', by which he meant that sentiment which is aroused in us when we see a fellow-being suffer. Whenever this happens, he held, we are filled with a desire to help because we ourselves are suffering as we watch the grief or pain of another; that is, we are, as it were, vicariously afflicted, and necessarily so, by other people's pains or sorrows.

By interpreting Cumberland's benevolence as 'sympathy' and using the latter term rather than the former, though not by any means in every passage of his work, Hume succeeded in removing the conflict between self-love and benevolence, which Cumberland had insisted on, while retaining Hobbes's basic doctrine, namely, that all human action has one motive only, self-interest. Benevolence, Hume teaches, is part of that sole motive force within us. However, of the various aspects of Hume's work his repeated assertion that moral action flows not from reason but from sentiment has attracted most attention, as well as most opposition. Hume's argument runs on the following lines: emotion is that property within us which seeks happiness and eschews misery. Reason can only analyse a situation and estimate the balance of happiness or unhappiness likely to result from any action we may take, but reason by itself can never *induce* action. It is merely a faculty of judging between what is good and useful and what is not, or what is better and more useful and what is less so. It is a separate faculty, existing side by side with our feelings and emotions.[1]

It appears that Hume had two objectives in mind as he argued in this manner. First, he attempted to refute the view that, since our passions prevented us from acting morally and reason alone could overcome our passions (as Descartes, Spinoza and others had maintained), moral action depended on the dominance of reason over passion. But secondly, and more important, he wished to overcome that dualism between body and soul which was the heritage of medieval thinking on ethical subjects and to which, as he observed, his contemporaries were clinging, unable to extricate themselves.

In this context, though in his earlier work, the *Treatise on Human Nature*, Hume made his celebrated remark about the logical fallacy he said he had often noticed, namely, the fallacy of gliding almost imperceptibly from an 'is'-proposition to an 'ought'-proposition, that is, from a sentence stating a fact to one containing a command.[2] By making this point and indeed giving it some emphasis, Hume was probably merely stating as clearly as he could that sentiment, not reason, prompted moral action and that it would be quite wrong to deduce moral obligations from any process of reasoning. In our time, however, Hume's remark about this particular fallacy has received a great deal of attention and has often been the subject of academic debate, as we shall see later when discussing recent and present-day English philosophy.

To illustrate what I said at the beginning, namely, that no one has written about ethics with a deeper understanding of man's moral nature than Hume, I will quote the following passage from the *Enquiry*:

The hypothesis which allows for a disinterested benevolence, distinct from self-love, has really more *simplicity* in it and is more conformable to the analogy of nature than that which pretends to resolve all friendship and humanity into this latter principle . . . Where is the difficulty in conceiving that, from the original frame

[1] 'Mere reasoning can never make us act; it is sentiment which drives us on to intervene and help—ourselves or others' (*An Enquiry concerning the Principles of Morals*, no. 246).

[2] *Treatise on Human Nature*, bk. 3, pt. 1, 1739–40.

of our temper we may feel a desire for another's happiness or good, which, by means of that affection becomes our own good, and is afterwards pursued from the combined motives of benevolence and self-enjoyment? Who sees not that vengeance, from the force alone of passion, may be so eagerly pursued, as to make us knowingly neglect every consideration of ease, interest or safety; and like some vindictive animals, infuse our very souls into the wounds we give an enemy; and what a malignant philosophy must it be that will not allow to humanity and friendship the same privileges which are indisputedly granted to the darker passions of enmity and resentment?[1]

3. Kant's ethics is pre-eminent. It combines two qualities which most philosophers have found it almost impossible to reconcile, complexity and consistency. It is complex because it reflects the influence not only of Greek and post-Renaissance views but also of medieval thinking, which Kant reinterpreted in Enlightenment terms. It is consistent in that it is dominated by two conceptions: (a) autonomy or freedom, and (b) the formalism of the moral law.

Kant begins his *Foundations of a Metaphysics of Morals* by saying that 'nothing can be said to be good without qualification except Good Will'. In saying this he may appear to be following Hume and his predecessors, who ascribed both selfishness and benevolence to man's nature as a whole; but, on the contrary, markedly deviating from the English philosophers, he goes on to teach that the Good Will does not belong to man as a creature of nature but stems from something higher, indeed the divine element in man, and is merely the empirical reflex of an *a priori* faculty, practical reason.[2] With

[1] *Enquiry*, appendix II, nos. 253 and 254. Here Hume implicitly rejects Hobbes's doctrine that self-love excludes all non-selfish action and that we act 'unselfishly' only in order to obtain an advantage for ourselves.

[2] Kant has coined the term moral theology (Moraltheologie), A 632 = B 660, to characterize his own approach to the relation of ethics to theology. It reverses the scholastic doctrine on that relationship: whereas according to the medieval Church the existence of God makes it imperative for man to follow ethical rules, Kant teaches that it is the moral law within us which proves the existence of the Deity. Kant describes the proposition 'God exists' as a postulate of practical reason. Clearly, Kant's use of the term 'postulate' differs from that of his predecessors and—one may add—successors. In Kant's conception a postulate is an inferential proposition in a mode different from the mode of the premises on which that proposition is based, i.e. the postulate of the existence of God (an 'is-proposition') is based on the moral law (an 'ought-proposition').

this teaching Kant returns to, even highlights, the medieval or religious division of man's nature into an earthly and a divine part, maintaining that on the one hand man as part of nature (animate and inanimate) is subject to nature's causal laws, sharing his basic impulses with brutes and beasts, and to that extent is actuated by self-love only, and on the other that the divine element with which he is also endowed enables him to rise above his empirical impulses and 'obtain freedom from the mechanism of nature',[1] that is to say, is able to overcome the animal instinct of self-love and act as pure practical reason commands.

It is in this ability to act against, or in spite of, nature that man's *freedom* consists; and since man is free in this sense, it is possible to ascribe autonomy to the human will, that is, man's ability to legislate for himself. And since pure practical reason prescribes the moral law, autonomy also means that man imposes that law, or the 'categorical imperative', as Kant calls it, on himself. In other words man demands of himself that he should follow the ethical rule as the supreme guiding principle of his actions.

As one looks for models of the Kantian concept of 'autonomy', it is apparent at once that it is analogous to the concept of divine autonomy (God's goodness), which is part not only of scholastic but also of Renaissance teaching; and that Kant aims at transferring the extraneous influence of the Deity to man's own faculty of practical reason. Moreover, going further back, Kant's autonomy owes a great deal to Stoic philosophy, and in particular to the Stoic notion of the *logos*, which, however, in Stoic teaching works *within nature*.

In conformity with his main conclusion, namely, that it is practical reason which gives the moral law to man, Kant argues that moral action must have no other motive than that of obeying the command of reason, thereby exercising his freedom over nature or rather over his own natural impulses, which would always merely make him seek pleasure and avoid pain. Kant is very emphatic on this point: happiness, *eudaimonia*, he says, or the seeking of it, is the very opposite of the ethical demand. It is this aspect of his teaching for which Kant was criticized, and even ridiculed, in his own time and has been ever since. Must I hate doing a good deed,

---

In common usage 'postulate' simply means 'hypothesis in need of being verified'.

[1] *Critique of Practical Reason*, p. 155 in the original edition.

it was asked, for this good deed to be morally admirable? Am I not allowed to enjoy being kind, or gladly to do a friend a good turn? Still, Kant maintains his position with the utmost rigour and rejects any moral philosophy which incorporates the attainment of happiness in its doctrines.

But in spite of all criticism Kant's ethics has exercised a powerful influence not only on all subsequent philosophers but on education in general and on conduct. The influence of Kant's moral philosophy, as might be expected, was strongest in Kant's own country, Prussia and later in Imperial Germany. The categorical imperative, not perhaps in its strictly philosophical sense but generally as a command to be upright and act honestly in whatever circumstances, was accepted as the universal guide of behaviour rather than religious teaching, because it was far more in tune with the spirit of the late eighteenth and nineteenth centuries, an age which prided itself on its humanistic and secular culture. The imperative was instilled in young people's minds in the schools and the home, and as they grew up was passed on by them to the next generation. Moreover Kant's teaching suited the Prussian governing authorities because Kant praised the fulfilment of duty above all other moral actions. Kant found that the concept of duty epitomized all that his imperative was to convey; and it was duty that the Prussian authorities proclaimed as the principle by which their citizens should always be guided. For to do one's duty meant acting in a certain way, whether or not such action was in accordance with one's own desires, and indeed more often than not duty was likely to run counter to what one would have preferred to do. Kant may be said to have composed almost a hymn to duty.[1] He describes duty as an end in itself and the command to do one's duty as one coming from a transcendent source. Its opposite is inclination, which belongs to the natural world; and indeed Kant goes so far as to say that it is the lot of ordinary people to do their duty against their will or desire—that is, unhappily—and that one can only expect a saint to do his duty gladly.

This Kantian conclusion has been criticized, as has also his rigorous insistence on absolute truthfulness. For Kant says that you must not lie to someone who intends to murder a person if he asks you about the whereabouts of his intended victim, even though you are aware of the purpose of his question. Kant's stern inflexibility

[1] Ibid., pp. 154f.

3

was attacked by many.[1] Yet he would not be moved from his position. He felt that no empirical emotion—not even pity or charity—could possibly rank equally with the transcendent and absolute moral command.

Nevertheless it cannot be said that Kant was trying to please the monarch whose subject he was, the king of Prussia, though he was no doubt partly influenced by the spirit of the Prussian administration in which, *inter alia*, corruption was not tolerated and, if uncovered, was punished with great severity, especially when it occurred in the civil service. Kant's ethics, it is true, is the ethics of a citizen living in a stable society and on the whole in a well-governed state, and hence it is an ethics concerned with the relations of individual citizens to one another under state laws which remained unquestioned; it contains no discussions of the relation of a citizen to the state, let alone of the citizen's right to reform the state, or indeed rebel against it or its ruler. Yet in spite of his silences Kant implies that on the basis of his teaching the ethical command stands higher than obedience to the state or a government's decrees. He does not demand rebellion against immoral orders or laws, nor even open opposition, but he expects tacit non-cooperation. Kant gives a telling example of what he has in mind in the *Methodenlehre of the Critique of Practical Reason*, referring to what alas! is so familiar in our time but was uncommon in his own age and country. Taking for his illustration an episode from English history, Kant explains what in his view an upright man should have done and suffered at the time of the Reformation when Henry VIII put Anne Boleyn to death—an action deeply deplored by the German Protestants of Henry's time and in particular by Melanchthon.[2] That is to say, Kant felt that even at the risk of their lives the Protestants should not have cooperated with the king as he carried out his cruel policy. In short, Kant did not counsel rebellion, he called for martyrdom.

The second significant feature of Kant's ethics is its 'formalism'.

[1] Recently, Gerhard Funke has ably defended Kant against this charge, by arguing that Kant teaches *respect* for the moral law rather than an inflexible obedience to it, which—as Funke points out—would make of Kant the advocate of an 'impersonalism' amounting to pure, perfect unselfishness. On the contrary, according to Funke, Kant's ethics does not imply that our respect for the moral law excludes our desire for, or attainment of, happiness (*Kant-Studien*, vol. 65, special issue, pt. I, pp. 45ff. 1974).

[2] *Critique of Practical Reason*, pp. 277f.

Formalism in an ethical context means that it is impossible to characterize the moral law in any other way than by describing it as universally applicable; much as the logical laws are universally or generally valid independently of any particular object to which they may be made to refer. To prove that the ethical rule can only be conceived in a formal way, Kant mainly argues that it is impossible to derive it from man's intentions because, he says, all human intentions are directed towards some material object for the purpose of holding and using or enjoying it.[1] All such intentions, and all actions flowing from them, belong to the animal side of man's nature; and whatever they may be aimed at, their motives can always be reduced to one impulse, that of self-love, and the craving for happiness, *eudaimonia*.[2] Kant concludes that because all human intentions are caused by material objects they are unsuited to be used in the search for ethical rules, and equally matter itself can never be the source of moral maxims. Therefore ethical enquiry must confine itself to the search for a universal *form* to which all intentions, motives and actions, if they are to be morally right or of a moral character, must be subject. This form Kant believed he had found. It is his celebrated *categorical imperative:* 'Always act in such a manner that the maxim of your intentions could become the principle of a general legislation.' Or: 'Act on a maxim which you can will to be law universal' (Sidgwick).

Kant teaches further that, since this imperative is not derived from any desire for objects, nor therefore from anything material at all, but on the contrary is capable of overcoming selfish desires, it is non-material, i.e. belongs to the divine side of man's nature, or in Kantian terms stems from pure practical reason, which of course is within man and, although it acts in every individual as that individual's own reason (or conscience), is common to all human beings or even to all rational beings and therefore *a priori* and permanent, eternal. And completing his enquiry Kant states that practical reason is concerned with two concepts only: the morally good and the morally bad; the good as the object to be sought, the bad as the object to be avoided, rejected.

Having reached this point, Kant repudiates the moral views of all his predecessors on the grounds that they are based on material principles and not, as his own ethics is, on a formal rule. For as he

[1] Doctrine 1, ibid., p. 38.
[2] Ibid., p. 40.

has stressed before, happiness in its most commonly used sense is bound up with the attainment of a material object, and on these grounds it is easy for Kant to refute any kind of philosophy which may be called hedonistic: the Epicurean, which, according to Kant seeks happiness in emotional, sensuous and physical pleasure; the views of Montaigne who recommended cheerfulness through the enjoyment of the society of one's fellow-men; the opinion of Mandeville, who makes the prosperity of a society dependent less on the virtues than on the selfish ambitions of its members; and the theory of Hutchison who, as Kant believed, taught that gratification of the moral sense was the aim of ethical behaviour. But Kant not only denounced these views as ethically invalid or mistaken, but he also criticized the Stoic doctrine of happiness through the achievement of perfect virtue as heterogeneous to true Ethics, that is to say, as derived from a non-ethical root, the desire for happiness. Finally, he even attacked the religious way of teaching morality, as being bound to material objectives. For religion too, Kant implies, makes happiness its aim, since it wishes us to believe that those who fulfil God's will are sure to enjoy perfect peace of mind in this world and a blessed life hereafter.[1]

The introduction of 'formalism' into ethics is Kant's own great contribution to moral philosophy. None of the earlier philosophers had thought of it and very few have taken up his lead. Accordingly, in spite of the general admiration which his philosophy has always enjoyed, the formalism of his ethics has often been criticized, even by his admirers. For example, the German historians of philosophy and later the advocates of a material-value-ethics—quite apart from those who disputed his standpoint as a whole, that is to say, the ethical relativists—have disputed not only his ethical formalism as such but also the manner in which he considered it best to give expression to it, namely, the categorical imperative. The imperative, it has been remarked, is in essence 'banal and commonplace' because in philosophical language it merely restates the familiar old saying: 'Do not do to others what you do not wish others to do to you.' It has also been argued that when you are directed to act in accordance with Kant's formal principle it is implied that you should act in that way because you do not want the world to dissolve into chaos; an implication which is factual, empirical, material. In other words, the imperative is based on the supposition that you want a

[1] Ibid., pp. 69ff.

firm social order in the part of the world where you live, and presumably the existing order, to be smoothly maintained. Indeed the examples given by Kant himself reinforce this argument.[1] All such objections can be summarised as follows: the imperative presupposes that you want the world to be well regulated, so that you can live in it happily or at least undisturbed; that is, it implies not only empirical representations but also selfish motives.

Nevertheless all such criticism is basically groundless. It misses the central issue. For although it is right to argue that material purposes are included or hidden in Kant's moral imperative and, beyond this, that any wording or phrasing of an imperative, even if it is meant to be purely formal, must relate somehow to matter, it has to be realized that the continuance of the world in which we live is merely a necessary assumption underlying what one could describe as a *test-yourself-formula*, which Kant has devised and expressed in the shape of his imperative.

And on those same grounds Kant's formalism as such has been attacked. Pure formalism, it has been said, is illusory and false because any ethical command must relate to objects or facts, and hence there can be no formal precept without some material content. But even though this general criticism of Kant's formalism has greater weight than any criticism directed against the wording of his imperative, it should be understood that, when Kant advises us to examine the moral quality or otherwise of any action we consider taking, or to ask ourselves whether or not the maxim on which our action is based could become a universal rule of conduct, what he aims at is solely to find a rule applicable to, but independent of, changing circumstances and usable in any situation which may arise and in which you may consider taking one action or another. Therefore it does not contravene the purely formal character of Kant's imperative in the sense in which it should be understood: as a methodical device by which the ethical rule becomes universally applicable.

In Kantian terms, the moral command is *a priori*, that is to say, it comes from a higher source than man's natural impulses, which are *empirical*; and, however surprising it may appear to a scientist, the higher command can over-rule all empirical causes or motives of behaviour. However, we do not have to accept Kant's concepts of the *a priori* or the *empirical* nor his explanation of man's dual

[1] Ibid., pp. 49f.

nature, expressed by him through the distinction between sense on the one hand and reason on the other, to agree to his essential teaching, namely, that the rule of ethical conduct, however formulated, is independent of varying world conditions—self-based, autonomous and unchanging.

It is commonly assumed that Kant has expressed the moral law as he conceived it in two versions: first, as the categorical imperative, and secondly, by saying that every person should be treated as an end in itself and never merely as a means to an end.[1]

By restating Kant's reflections in the form of a command, viz. 'Never treat another person as merely an instrument but always as an end in itself', commentators have transformed Kant's additional explanation of his ethical theory into what amounts to a second imperative. Kant himself, however, evidently did not mean this second precept as either an alternative to his imperative or even as its equivalent. Nevertheless it has often been so regarded, and indeed frequently far more highly praised, than the imperative itself, because it seemed to confirm and reinforce the *ethics of personality* which was so much favoured during the nineteenth and early twentieth centuries.

Kant himself explains how he arrived at his second rule as follows. Practical reason, the source of the moral law, he says, resides in every person. Hence the dignity which practical reason confers on man must be respected in every individual, no matter what his personal qualities—commendable or otherwise—may be, It is interesting to observe how in this context Kant uses the word *heilig* in two senses, saintly and sacred. The average person, he says, is certainly by no means *saintly*; yet every human being is *sacred* however he may behave, insofar as he carries a divine element, the moral law, within him.[2]

Whereas Kant explains on what philosophical premisses his second precept is based, he does not reveal what he may have had in mind when he decided to incorporate it in his ethical teaching. For although one may argue that the second rule is universally valid and deals with all relationships between human beings which may occur anywhere and at any time, on further and deeper reflection it becomes clear that to use another person as a means to an end—although this may often enough occur within the family, between

---

[1] Ibid., pp. 155ff.
[2] Ibid.

parents and children, brothers and sisters, or between friends—it is most frequently observed (a) in the master–servant relation, and (b) above all, in the way governments act against their citizens. For when Kant says that not even God is 'allowed' to treat a human being as a mere means to an end, he wishes to convey, while stating his view with the utmost caution, that no one, neither king nor priest, is permitted in the name of God to treat a man as a mere means to an end; and that as regards the individual he should rather let himself be martyred than be so used. As pointed out before, whereas Kant does not advocate rebellion, he certainly expresses his admiration for those who choose to die for their convictions rather than participate in wicked deeds.[1]

There is yet another angle to this so-called second version of the imperative. Some religiously influenced teachers of ethics have preached that to suffer for a sacred cause brings with it happiness, bliss. Kant, however, who is always intent on excluding happiness from ethics, is at pains to point out that martyrdom does not lead to bliss or happiness; on the contrary. But he does say that the martyred person will derive some *comfort* from contemplating that he suffers torture or death because he has done his duty. As is well known, in Beethoven's opera *Fidelio* Floristan in his first aria sings 'A sweet comfort remains for me: it consists in my knowledge that I have done my duty.'

There is one more comment which I think it is fair to make. Governments, whether monarchical or democratic, have often treated the inhabitants of conquered territories without regard to their dignity. This happened in Kant's own time. So, as one considers this implication of his teaching, it becomes evident once again that, even if he does not say so openly, and though he apparently writes solely for the citizen who lives peacefully with other citizens under an unchallenged, respected law, he is deeply aware of the necessity to make both individuals and governments acknowledge the validity of the moral law and with it the dignity of the person.

---

[1] See Friedrich Kaulbach's valuable contribution to an understanding of the relation between the moral law and state law in Kant's ethical writings (*Kant-Studien*, vol. 67, 3, pp. 390ff. 1976).

D. The Nineteenth Century

1. In nineteenth-century moral philosophy several aspects of pre-Kantian ethics came to the fore once more: the views (1) that all human action including moral action is motivated by self-interest, (2) that happiness is the aim of all human action, and (3) that ethics and politics, that is, individual conduct and society law or custom, are closely linked to each other.

However, a romantic element was now added to earlier opinions: it was thought that a near-perfect relation between the individual and his community was capable of being achieved. One school in particular devoted its strength and energy to the discovery and clarification of this relation, the school of the Utilitarians, among whom Jeremy Bentham was the outstanding thinker, with Godwin preceding and James Mill following him. In regarding self-interest as the mainspring of human action, the Utilitarians followed in the tradition mainly of Hobbes but also of Hutchison and Hume. But unlike Hobbes, they were not content with merely proving that self-interest demanded consideration for others as well as oneself. Rather, inspired by the French Revolution and by the writers who prepared the ground for that great event, in particular Rousseau, they tried not only, like Hobbes, to preserve society as it was but to improve and reform it. Influenced by Rousseau's doctrine of the 'general will' (about which more will be said presently) but slightly varying it, Bentham taught that the individual's *happiness* was linked to the happiness of his fellow-men. He elaborated this view by pointing out that general progress towards happiness benefits the individual, who contributes towards it, in a twofold way: it gives him an inner gratification, which is the same as happiness, and secondly, in common with every other individual, he profits by the general raising of living standards within his community. Bentham concludes (a) that an individual cannot be happy unless most other people belonging to his community are also happy, and (b) that everybody's own happiness is increased in proportion to the growing happiness of as many as possible of his fellow-men. The famous formula in which he expressed his aim was: the greatest happiness of the greatest number.

In other words, the happiness of the individual and the happiness of the community are one and the same. As mentioned Bentham was influenced by Rousseau's conception of the general will. Since this conception has lately been much debated, I should like to devote a few words to its interpretation. Its basis is Rousseau's conviction that a community exists for the benefit not of its master but of all its members. Hence he argues that the will of all, the general will, is the will of each of the members of this community, because they are all motivated by the same interest, namely, the well-being of the community, which must be reflected in each person's own well-being. He further argues that to exercise one's own will for one's own benefit, which is also the community's benefit, means to exercise one's will freely, and so, in Rousseau's view, a person's freedom consists in his ability to exercise his own will. Since Rousseau lived in a monarchical state and knew that his views were revolutionary, he added a sentence which is now frequently criticized, namely, that 'if necessary men have to be forced to be free'. It is this sentence which has been held against Rousseau, because, as modern critics have said, it implies that he was in fact advocating totalitarianism because he wished—so they say—a majority to suppress a minority within a community. It seems to me, however, that such critics do not take into account the historic circumstances under which Rousseau wrote, nor do they understand what he really meant to convey, namely, that people have to be delivered from their bondage to tradition,[1] or made to abandon their habit of obeying a master, in order to be free, that is, to follow their own inclination, which they will never do except to further their own interest and serve their own benefit.

By making common progress his primary objective rather than the improvement of the individual, Bentham has exercised an influence which it is impossible to overrate on all subsequent social changes. Not only much of the legislation enacted in the nineteenth century but such twentieth-century innovations as social security, unemployment benefits and the health service have their origin in Bentham's work—his theory *and* his practice, because he was for ever striving to have his plans implemented by government. Bentham is therefore deservedly renowned. Besides, the history of the effects of Bentham's thought (as of Rousseau's and Marx's) prove that, whereas thought by itself will, in small measure and perhaps almost imperceptibly, transform society, and in fact often

---

[1] People are freed from long-established traditions by great events and changing views in their wake.

has, it is only through political action on a large scale that new ideas can have a powerful, decisive impact on a nation or on mankind. More will be said on this theme later.

Bentham believed that the progress that the community and its members were to make together was linked to the advance which science and industry were continually making in his time. Discovery and inventions were to be harnessed to the well-being of all mankind, and thus the two greatest evils which beset all communities, and so many of their members—poverty and disease—would be overcome.

Bentham was a jurist, and it has sometimes been said that he had no philosophy of his own but merely gave a new administrative dimension and aim to a certain type of ethics, which was already well-known and had become a tradition especially in his own country. But Bentham did not think of himself as a philosopher in the traditional sense of the word; and perhaps in deliberate opposition to Kant, who excluded happiness altogether from moral philosophy, he regarded himself as an (ethical) materialist, an Epicurean, that is, a non-metaphysical, non-religious thinker. He believed that happiness was the goal of all human action and in elaborating the notion of happiness he maintained (like Spinoza) that it consisted solely in the attainment of pleasure and the avoidance of pain. At this point he introduced the term 'utility', defining it as the means of achieving pleasure and averting pain; and of course it is from this term and its definition that he and his school have received their name—Utilitarians.

Having appreciated Bentham's greatness, which lies in the close link he forged between the interests of the individual and the interests of most of his fellow-men, we must make some critical remarks. Though Bentham did not aim at Utopia—as he said expressly several times—but at progress and reform, he took too lofty a view of the individual's concern with society or the community in which he lived. It is true he did not ignore the jealousy, rivalry and hatred which arise between one individual and another and with which earlier ethical philosophy had been concerned, but he seemed to believe that, as compared with the strength of the bond which unites all individuals within a community, their discords and struggles against each other were insignificant. Bentham appears to have overlooked the fact that there exist within a society not only individuals but groups—strata—which were soon to be called *classes*; and he did not foresee that these classes, far from happily collaborating, would set themselves up against one another. Or, if he did foresee this development he may have believed that the interests of the nation would always prove stronger than those of any groups within the nation. After all, his was the era of nationalism. And exactly as he believed that the individual's main desire was to improve his lot, so he may have thought that a nation as a whole was principally intent on improving its own wealth, power and influence in the world in competition with other nations.

2. Bentham had insisted that the happiness of the individual and the happiness of people at large were one and the same, and it was precisely on this issue that John Stuart Mill (the son of James Mill), who at an early age had been designated Bentham's successor, broke away from utilitarianism. Bentham had failed to recognize, J. S. Mill felt, that each individual seeks his own kind of happiness or has his own conception of the 'good'; and from this he went on to assert that, if the 'good' of society was to be achieved, each individual must be free to realize his own 'good', in other words that that society was best in which as many individuals as possible did *not* simply accept the general 'good' as their own 'good'. Evidently Mill criticized utilitarianism because it gave inadequate consideration to the individual's most elementary right, that is, the right to be himself or to be free to develop his potential strength, whether physically or intellectually. And so, while basically remaining Bentham's disciple—regarding happiness as the goal of all human action—Mill endeavoured to design a doctrine which, he hoped, would safeguard the individual's essential rights without endangering society as a whole. His conclusion, published in his *Essay on Liberty*, was that each individual should be free to think and act as he considered right, so long as he would allow the same freedom of thought and action to everybody else; in other words, that the individual should be free as long as his own freedom did not encroach on the freedom of any of his fellow-men. Mill expressed his doctrine by coining a new phrase or rather by creating a new concept, that of the 'sovereignty of the individual'— a significant term, because it confers upon the individual what used to be the sole prerogative of the state. It meant that Mill gave the individual the right to legislate for himself while taking away

from society, or a section of society, the right to legislate for all.

A reader may well ask at this point, What is society? Is it simply an abstract term with a meaning too vague and varied adequately to be defined in a general way? Though this may be so, one may try to delineate the notion of society from a (historically) fixed standpoint: Society consists of a number of people who set themselves up as judges and once they have formed a judgement, by whatever process, expect that everybody belonging to their society must comply with it. In fact this was the generally practised and acknowledged function of society in Mill's time—the function which Mill found unacceptable. Therefore he thought it necessary to seek a way by which to make the individual, the eccentric and even the heretic as respectable as society itself, or at least completely unassailable. And this he wished to achieve all the more because he was a fully accepted member of the society into which he was born and therefore was particularly vulnerable to the penalties which society seemed entitled to inflict, namely, unfavourable judgements, ostracisms and so on.

With the freedom of the individual in mind, Mill describes as the principal aim of his *Essay* the determination of the limits of rightful interference by society with the individual's freedom (ch. 1) and also of the penalties that society may justly impose on the individual's life (ch. 4).

In the introduction to his *Essay*, Mill emphatically states that he does not wish to attack any particular aspect of the suppression of the individual in the book (though in other books he does direct his attack against particular 'injustices' inflicted by society—for instance, in restricting the freedom of women to develop their own potential) but that he is concerned with the freedom of the individual in a general way.

Since Mill is so much concerned with the individual's right to feel, think and speak as he wishes, it is evident that the emphasis of his doctrine falls on man's private life; and since Mill imposes a strict ban on anyone's right to interfere with the freedom of anybody else, Mill in effect seems to make it impossible for a person to bring about a change in social structure. For change, and in particular revolutionary change, certainly makes interference at least with some people's rights—their property, their privileges, that is to say their freedom—inevitable. And yet, since, somewhat inconsistently, Mill makes freedom of speech one of the most important rights of each individual and beyond that a prerequisite of probing the truth about a fact or the validity of a view, it is clear that Mill's philosophy is not altogether confined to the area of private experience but has a public side to it too. Indeed retrospectively it appears that Mill's insistence on full freedom of discussion (*audiatur et altera pars*) is precisely that aspect of Mill's work which has had the deepest and most lasting influence on English thinking and habits till today.

3. This seems to be a suitable point—and not only for chronological reasons—to devote some attention to 'Darwinism', that is, to the general influence exercised by, or the broader consequences stemming from, Darwin's famous theory of the gradual evolution of the human species from the lower forms of animal life.

It is true of course that long before Darwin people had realized and stated that life was a continuous fight for survival and that each individual had to struggle in order to go through it safely or at least relatively unharmed. The celebrated, or notorious saying that 'might is right' goes back to the Greeks. Still never before Darwin had it been said that the species of civilized man owed its existence to the suppression or elimination of weaker species or even of the weaker members of the human species itself; that is, that only the fittest of a species survive. By implication this meant that the next evolutionary phase could only come about in the same way, namely, through the victory of the strong over the weak. As a result, ethically speaking, it became a virtue to be strong and a duty to be merciless, because in no other way could the species be preserved, and its improvement could be secured only by the increasing power and utter ruthlessness of the strong.

It is almost impossible to overrate the impact that Darwinism has had, not only on scientists but on the general public. The notion that each of us must choose to be either 'hammer' or 'anvil' took hold of the minds of all but a few; and these few were regarded, and often ridiculed, as otherworldly, 'saintly'. Conversely moral exhortations or warnings were no longer taken seriously, and indeed were derided by a considerable majority of people as outdated and contrary to the truths of life as superseded by science.

On the face of it, then, it is difficult to see what Darwinism has to do with moral philosophy, in the traditional sense of the term. Still one famous thinker, Nietzsche, who though he would never have admitted that his philosophy was an outgrowth of Darwin's theories and in fact brought to Darwinism a wealth of deep and inspired thought of his own, made of it something akin to a moral philosophy. But before we can discuss Nietzsche in detail we must turn to another philosopher or theologian of the nineteenth century who, incidentally, like Nietzsche, was one of the great influences on existentialism—Kierkegaard.

4. Whereas in England the importance of society was not deprecated even by those who, like Mill, championed the freedom of the individual within his community, on the continent thinking about the relationship between the individual and society developed on different lines. The individual under the term 'personality' was raised to ever greater heights, whereas correspondingly the esteem in which society was held was progressively lowered. What in England continued to be called society became 'the masses' in Europe, the common herd from which 'personality' would inevitably strive to detach itself completely. One of the first who led philosophers and the educated public in general along those ways of thinking was Kierkegaard. Resuscitating once again the division of man into a divine and animal element, he gave each individual, on the strength of his divine component, the right of an absolutely free choice in all matters, particularly in matters of moral relevance. There are no objective standards of a moral kind, he held, and what theories have been devised in the past to prove that objective standards do exist are in fact mere disguises of the truth, which is, that our moral decisions are our own. Each personality, according to Kierkegaard, chooses his ethical standard and aim. Kierkegaard thus introduced arbitrariness into moral philosophy, a quality which he regarded as the supreme characteristic of the deity and hence equally of the divine part in man.

Kierkegaard expounded his theory, in *Fear and Trembling*, on the basis of a biblical text, the story of Abraham's readiness to sacrifice his own son by the command of God. And so it is easy to see that Kierkegaard meant to convey that God's decrees were not only inscrutable, as had been said for a long time, but, contrary to *human* reason, 'irrational'; and this quality of the 'irrational' came to be a significant factor in nineteenth- and twentieth-century thinking, for it was regarded by Kierkegaard as the most important single property of the individual, with dangerous and indeed tragic results. Kierkegaard certainly succeeded in implanting the spirit of the irrational in theology[1] and in ontology. Indeed he made it possible for ontology, which had been discredited by Kant, to be revived—by the existentialist philosophers.

5. It is doubtful whether Nietzsche was acquainted with the works of Kierkegaard, which in their own time were little known outside Denmark. He certainly knew Darwin; he even composed a poem in which he compared Darwin (unfavourably) with Goethe. There is a direct link between Darwin's theory of the survival of the fittest and Nietzsche's famous notion of the 'superman'. For the superman represents the next, or even the final, phase in the evolution of the human species. He is the individual—'personality'—who is conscious of his power to legislate for himself (J. S. Mill) and of his arbitrary right to choose (Kierkegaard); and for this reason he is stronger than, and superior to, the common herd, because the people in general are not aware of their right to legislate for themselves and, *a fortiori*, never exercise that right. The superman is certainly regarded by Nietzsche as fit to survive not only the envy and hatred but, if necessary, the onslaught of the masses which he despises; but whether in Nietzsche's view the world will be inhabited by the species 'superman' in the end, or whether the masses will have learned to disregard their traditional values and, instead of obeying their established authorities, will follow the superman of their own generation, is not quite clear.

It is evident from what has been said that Nietzsche's philosophy is ethics not in the constructive, but the negative, sense. He rejects all known forms of ethics and in particular tries to convince his fellow-men that their existing religiously inspired moral standards are false; and he attributes their origin to Christian teaching. It is well-known that Nietzsche described conventional ethics as the 'morality of slaves', and hence called on the people of his time to wake up and be themselves, removing from their way all that impeded their growth or prevented them from reaching greater heights. Indeed, Nietzsche repudiates not only the Christian virtues of obedience and humility but also justice and, above all, pity. Pity, according to Nietzsche, means support for the weak who, he

[1] See Rudolph Otto, *The Idea of the Holy*.

thinks, should be brushed aside or pushed under and not helped. Pity, Nietzsche says, is close to contempt; and he believes that Christ died because he loved and pitied the masses. For the masses did not want to be pitied, and regarding Christ's pity for them as contempt they crucified him.[1] His own—Zarathustra-Nietzsche's—pity, however, is militant contempt, which means that Nietzsche felt sure that *he* would not be martyred but triumph in the end.

All Nietzsche's works, and in particular *Thus spake Zarathustra*, are essentially comments on contemporary events and trends—perversions, as Nietzsche saw them. In that famous somewhat artificial, yet eminently readable, semi-prophetic style of his, which he had developed for *Zarathustra*, Nietzsche scorned the complacency of the citizens of the newly-founded German empire, their anxiety to please authority, their love of the good life, their 'waking sleep'. No doubt Nietzsche also owes a great deal to an earlier writer, who was well known, Heinrich Heine, and in particular to Heine's easy, flowing style, his liberalism in politics and his sarcasm. As to detail, Nietzsche criticizes many aspects of the contemporary scene with acute perception. For instance, of the historians or scholars of his time he said that they had become masks, which enacted the figures of the past and thereby completely lost their own selves. Of the positivists and scientists he remarked that what they considered to be real (in an empirical sense) was so shallow that it ceased even to be real.[2] He turned against Schopenhauer because Schopenhauer's 'will' was paralysed by pessimism, whereas Nietzsche's will, the 'Will to Power', was a conquering force certain of its victorious future.

E. *Modern Ethics*

1. No notice, or hardly any, was taken of Nietzsche's writings when they appeared; still less were they considered contributions to moral philosophy, even by the few who read them. On the other hand, ethical thought in the accepted sense of the word did find new expressions both in England and on the continent from the middle

---

[1] *Thus Spake Zarathustra* I, 3. At least this is what I make of this section.
[2] Ibid. II, *Vom Lande der Bildung*.

or end of the nineteenth century; and it is not too difficult to divide
the moral philosophy which has developed since then, and has
remained valid till today,[1] into four main categories:

(1) *A priori* ethics
(2) Intuitionist ethics
(3) Ethical relativism
(4) Moral scepticism.

There are several subdivisions as well as overlaps within these
categories. Not only sociological thinking but also linguistic philosophy are forms of ethical relativism, and logical-positivist ethics,
of scepticism. That there are some overlaps between these types of
ethics and their sub-types will be seen later.

2. Of the schools referred to, only the philosophers belonging
to those of the first category followed the (German) idealistic
tradition, by attempting to establish permanent and universal moral
values, though with a significant change of outlook. In direct
opposition to Kant, who taught that the moral command could only
be grasped as a legislative form, modern thinkers tried to discover
material *a priori* values. Pre-eminent among them was Max Scheler,[2]
a disciple of Husserl, the founder of the phenomenological school.
Scheler not only disputed Kant's contention that the ethical *a priori*
was exclusive to formalism, but even denied that it was fruitfully
compatible with pure legislative form.

As Husserl himself had attempted to isolate the *a priori logical*
forms within human consciousness, which he believed to be the only
true source of knowledge, so Scheler tried to discover the ethical
'values' within consciousness. To this end he employed Husserl's
method. That is to say, he conducted a phenomonological enquiry,
which (as regards ethics) consisted in the description of value-
setting-acts rather than in the analysis of the values themselves.[3]
Like Husserl himself and the phenomenological school as a whole,
he believed that what could be intuited within consciousness was

---

[1] 'To some extent, we are all still in the nineteenth century.' A. MacIntyre,
A Short History of Ethics, London 1966, p. 243.
[2] Max Scheler, *Der Formalismus in der Ethik und die materiale Wertethik*, in
Jahrbuch für Philosophie und phänomenologische Forschung, ed. E. Husserl, vol. 1,
2, Halle 1913. See especially pp. 446, 484f., 564f.
[3] See vol. 1, 1, p. 446 for Scheler's phenomenological methods.

4

permanent, universal and *a priori*, and hence he judged that the values so discovered were in fact absolute. He concluded further that it was possible to determine an *a priori* scale of values, and on that scale he placed—to point to the top grades only—the noble, the beautiful and, ultimately, 'personality'; the pleasant being ranged below these highest grades.

Personality, as we have seen, was introduced into ethics by some of the nineteenth-century philosophers. J. S. Mill endowed the individual with 'sovereignty' within its own sphere; Kierkegaard endowed him with arbitrary power of choice, Nietzsche with the prerogative of moral legislation. Scheler emphasized the uniqueness of each 'individual'. Every human face deserves to be noted (Lichtenberg, *Aphorisms*) because it represents one of God's ideas, whereas words or the acts of people are only derivative and secondary. However, there is this difference between an individual in the common sense of the word and a personality: the latter is aware of his uniqueness by being conscious of himself as a unitary whole. But although Scheler placed personality as such highest on his scale, he carried his analysis still further, namely, by giving each personality its own rank. This he did by explaining that the higher or lower value of any particular personality depended on that personality's own standards of grading. For instance, a person who places intellectual or transcendent values above material values, and indeed saintliness above everything else, is himself to be valued highly, whereas a person preferring sensuous values deserves lesser esteem.[1]

It is easy to see now that Scheler's superior and highest values were those of the intellectual élite of his day, and one cannot help expressing surprise at his naiveté in asserting that those values were absolute and ascribing to them the phenomenological *a priori*. For the élite of his time placed the beautiful and the noble above the agreeable and the vulgarly enjoyable, while assigning to the concept of 'personality' all that they considered profound, and perhaps divine, in man, including the creative power of genius as expressed in music, art and literature. So Scheler, their philosopher, praised those very same values, while giving a semblance of scientific proof to his doctrines by strictly following the partly psychological, partly intuitional, method of the phenomenological school.

All the same, Scheler's thought is firmly embedded in the German

[1] Ibid., pp. 564f.

philosophical tradition. Like Kant, he strove to replace a religiously based ethics with a secular one but, unlike Kant, an ethics not of reason but of sentiment and in particular love of beauty. For he and other highminded people of his time perceived that the joy or ecstasy felt by religious people, as they worship the deity, could be experienced also by those who reverently contemplate a masterpiece of art. Similar emotions, they discovered, were evoked—elation, enthusiasm and even the mystic's self-identification with the creator—emotions which transport you above yourself; and although originally the substitution of the adoration of the Deity by that of beauty resulted from an intellectual process, it is to the attendant emotions that devotion to secular culture, instead of religious worship, owes its origin.

3. F. H. Bradley, an English philosopher who is usually described as a neo-Hegelian, also made personality the focal point of his philosophy, but in a more practical manner than Scheler. Not content with a vague formula, by which personality is described as an individual's consciousness of his own unique self, he tried to devise a criterion by which a person can discover whether he is in fact acting as a personality. According to Bradley, an individual realizes himself—namely, as a personality—by seeing to it that any decision he takes is a decision from the depth of his whole self. It need hardly be pointed out that existentialism is foreshadowed by this doctrine of Bradley's, as it is to some extent by Scheler's.[1]

4. Whereas the philosophers just referred to attempted yet again to design ethical theories on an *a priori* basis, the main current of the age moved in the opposite direction. Nourished from various sources—historical, sociological, positivist—moral philosophy assumed a relativistic and sceptical character. It is probably the sociological approach that has made the strongest impact on contemporary thinking. There exists an affinity between sociological ethics, which of course is empirical or *a posteriori*, and material value ethics: the concept of value belongs to both these types of moral philosophy, but with this difference, that the values are not

[1] In existentialist philosophy 'existing', as distinguished from merely 'being-in-the-world', means living in accordance with that force in oneself which transcends the mere self.

regarded as permanent or *a priori* in sociological ethics but, on the contrary, as emanating from 'society' which, far from being permanent, is continually changing. To be more explicit: the values established by a community, or even by a society within a community, are the values which any individual who belongs to this society whether by necessity or choice would regard as his own; and, as the values of his society are transient, so will his be.

The sociological approach is as old as the Sophists. 'Whatever is thought just and admirable in any city is regarded as just and admirable by the citizens of that city for so long as it is thought just and admirable in that city,' says Protagoras, as we have noted, in Plato's *Theaetetus* 167c.

And in our own time, the followers of Karl Marx believed that the moral values of an individual, generally speaking, depend on the social structure of his society and in particular on the class to which he belongs.

Widening Marx's doctrine, the sociologists hold that *all* intellectual activity is merely a response to the political or socio-economic community in which an individual finds himself and hence, *a fortiori*, that moral conceptions and valuations ultimately flow from society. Whereas this may be said to be the foundation of sociological philosophy, there is an additional subjective element to it. If an individual moves from one sphere to another or gains access to different social structures (*Gebilde*), he acquires the capacity to choose his moral stand and indeed does so, as it were, arbitrarily, that is, in accordance with his taste or wishes.

The sociological view of ethical values naturally received much support from anthropological and historical investigations. Actions regarded as right and proper in one country or continent are not considered so in another, e.g. the equality of men and women, opposition to a government in power, or even the drinking of wine. What is treated as a crime in certain countries is treated leniently in others. When one surveys the various epochs of history, the contrasts become even more striking. The casting out of unwanted children was believed to be virtuous at one time because it was thought that it was practised by parents who were conscious of their duty to the clan or tribe to which they belonged. Nowadays, of course, it would be considered a most detestable crime. Adultery, which carried the death penalty in many primitive or ancient countries and is condemned as a serious crime in the Koran, is generally condoned nowadays and at the peak of the romantic epoch was positively praised, as a reflection of true love and its triumph over stale convention. Whereas offering or accepting bribes was regarded as a crime meriting severe punishment at some time and in some places, it is now looked upon with complacency. For very many people believe that corruption is unavoidable in human society: therefore, if the next person practises it, why shouldn't I? Quacks offering to cure body or soul are despised in western Europe, except by a small minority, but in Africa they are held in high esteem as medicine men.

(a) It is the concept of value which provides a link between the sociologists' ethics and the most impressive moral philosophy of our time, that of Moore (*Principia Ethica*, 1903). It is true that Moore, like the sociologists and the idealists, searched for the ultimate source of values, but he started in a different way from them. He maintained that all previous philosophers had mistaken valuable things or facts, that is relative values, for value itself, which is the 'Good'. Thereby he stated emphatically that all his predecessors had committed what he called the 'naturalistic fallacy'. Moore's basic argument is that one cannot act morally unless one first knows what is good, or what the good is; and only after we have discerned the good by itself can we judge our own actions—past, present or under consideration—as to whether they are, or were, or will be, good—that is, decide, by reasoning, whether one's attitudes or actions are moral or immoral.

What is the 'good'? Moore's basic thesis is that, in any proper sense of the word definition, the good is undefinable, because whereas definitions are meant to refer to complex things the good is simple or atomic, and, whereas a proper definition must be based on dividing or analysing, the good is unanalysible. In short the good is unique in the same sense as a colour, for instance, yellow. Yellow, Moore says,[1] may be analysed by physicists or explained by them as a special kind of light vibrations, yet—he rightly continues—it is *not* those light vibrations which we mean when we say 'yellow'. We do not perceive them; what in fact occurs is that we are *struck* by the qualitative difference of the colour 'yellow' as compared with any other colour or generally any other property belonging to an object. And therefore Moore's ethics has been described as *moral*

[1] *Principia Ethica*, no. 10.

intuitionism (a term coined by Sidgwick and ascribed by MacIntyre to Locke and Richard Price as well as to Moore).

To understand Moore, it is necessary to consider the ethical theories which Moore wished to replace by his own. He himself gave a clear hint as to what he wished to eliminate from moral philosophy. This hint is contained in the phrase already referred to, the 'naturalistic fallacy': a fallacy which he tried to remove from ethical thought. However, the meaning he gave to this term is strange and complex. He emphatically rejected all attempts to derive the notion of the good, and with it any valid moral philosophy, not only from natural objects, the attainment of which might be felt to be desirable, such as pleasure or honour, or from any experience external or internal, for instance happiness caused by some physical or aesthetic enjoyment, such as a day by the sea or a visit to the opera, but also from reasoning or (spurious) metaphysics or (false) *a priori* insights into, or deductions of, the essence of the good.

It is surely strange to see Moore bracketing together such different moral theories as those of the hedonists and the Stoics, the English moralists including Hume and the transcendental thinkers such as Kant. His reason for doing so, however, was that he wished to establish with unshakeable firmness that the good could not be derived from anything beyond itself, i.e. anything extraneous or 'natural', a term which in his usage included all that exists in the world of objects and in the mind. On the contrary the good is unique: it is itself and nothing else. Rightly, therefore, has Moore's philosophy been called 'intuitionism', and to defend his method of discovering the good simply by contemplating it with his mind's eye, Moore pointed to the generally agreed view that axioms, such as *A* cannot be *B* and *not-B* at the same time, were known in this way and this way only, that is, by intuition.

Should one perhaps therefore conclude that axioms rather than a colour, 'yellow', have provided Moore with a model for his 'good'? But of course, whereas yellow, like the good, is a simple idea, axioms are propositions. Now axioms can be made plain and intelligible because they are statements, each consisting of a subject and a predicate; but the good cannot be so explained. Moreover the good is disadvantaged as compared with yellow in another respect too: you can make clear what you mean by 'yellow', viz. by pointing to a yellow object and then a red object and then again to the yellow object, and in doing so, by means of words or gesticulations, convey to another person what you mean by yellow; and of course we all know, simply by watching children as they grow up that it is possible and even easy to make the meaning of 'yellow' understood. But how can anyone make sure that what he means by the 'good' is the same as what someone else means by this word, or be assured that *his* meaning of the good is also someone else's meaning? It cannot be done: Moore's good is non-communicable.

After stating his view on the ultimate value, the good by itself, Moore turns to the values which occur in our experience. And, Moore teaches, it is by anticipating and judging the consequences of any action which we may take that we do, or do not, find the good in the world of experience. Since we can be assumed to desire the good, we shape our action and thereby future reality in accordance with the good; we do not derive the good from an anticipated, imagined future reality. That is to say, Moore does not commit the 'naturalistic fallacy' of extracting the good from an anticipated experience. There is rather a teleological element in Moore's reasoning at this point: by aiming at the good we cause it to exist or come into being.

Our judgement hinges on whether the consequences we foresee have, or do not have, intrinsic value. It is easy, Moore argues further, to intuit a single good inherent in the consequences of any action that we may have taken, and an assessment of this kind need not be a matter of doubt or dispute; but, according to Moore, grave problems arise when values are set against values. Of course these are problems which had also exercised the minds of many earlier philosophers—conflicts of duties, moral dilemmas—and no doubt with such conflicts in mind Moore stated his three rules of valuation: one has to decide, first, which of two values is the higher; secondly, which of two evils is the lesser; thirdly, whether the balance of a total of values and demerits belonging to a complex situation is, or is not, in favour of the good.[1]

As to the values themselves, Moore assigns the highest places (1) to the appreciation of beauty, and (2) to passions and affection. Evidently Moore shares his preference for these values with most of his intelligent contemporaries. Rather uncharitably MacIntyre has described Moore's values as 'private, parochial and class-bound'.[2] Moore himself introduces his high admiration of beauty

[1] Ibid., no. 17. [2] MacIntyre, *op. cit.*, p. 256.

by saying that 'it is universally agreed that the appreciation of a beautiful object is a good thing in itself'.[1]

In the last section of the book, to which he gives the title 'The Ideal', Moore stresses that his ethics is *not* an ethics of perfection. He does so by explaining what he means by 'The Ideal'. For Moore excludes from ethics any theory which makes the *summum bonum* an aim worth pursuing, whether it consists in a spiritual absolute, such as the contemplation of the universe in its harmony, or the vision of a world entirely different from that of our experience (as Kant does in his theory of the positive *noumenon*). As against such theories, Moore holds that material qualities are necessary constituents of the ideal in our kind of world;[2] and that no moral philosophy designed for man as he is should set up the absolute ideal or perfect virtue as its ultimate objective or as an aim capable of ever being achieved.

If we agree with Moore that it is impossible to define the good, we may still attempt to circumscribe, if not *the* good, at least a generally acceptable version of it.[3] To many people the morally good is found in pure unselfishness, whether in action or in attitude. Each of us may either have had or have imagined some experience of such an action or attitude. As regards the first, you may yourself either watch or imagine another forego a holiday which you or he has planned, to give the money set aside for the journey to a friend who happens to be in dire need of help. As to the second, you may yourself be or watch or imagine another person to be in an unfortunate situation, yet contemplate a neighbour's good fortune not with envy but with pleasure or a kind of vicarious joy.

In experiencing or imagining such an action or attitude you or I vividly receive two impressions or *immediate* ideas, namely, those of unselfish action and an unselfish attitude. By transferring these ideas to other actual or potential experiences of a similar kind we gain what may prove a central conception. For our next step is to search for morally relevant experiences and conceive them in such a way that in one sense or another, directly or indirectly, they reflect that basic or central conception which we have formed. Our purpose

---

[1] *Principia Ethica*, no. 114.

[2] Ibid., no. 123.

[3] It will be seen later that the 'better' is a more useful conception to form the basis of a modern ethics than the 'good'; cf. pp. 6of.

in so proceeding is to build up a consistent system of ethics. Although at some times critics have deprecated the value or importance of unitary systems, it is impossible to deny that a consistent argument relating to a subject has a greater force than a two-sided discussion of it or indeed a discussion from many, various, standpoints.

Of the notions which present themselves, justice, courage, sympathy and so on, may well be considered particularly relevant. Justice is usually defined as the right apportioning of shares among two or more people, irrespective of person or rank.[1] Viewed from our own central twin-concept, justice is such fair apportioning of shares amounting to an unselfish action flowing from an unselfish state of mind—the judge's. That is, the judge in this example neither acts corruptly nor is guided by personal preferences or dislikes.

Or take courage. A courageous deed is the action of a person who when he or others are threatened exposes himself to (mortal) danger. It is also the action of an individual who being dependent on a superior's favour acts in defiance of his superior because of a deep-felt conviction. The first is an example of physical, the second of mental courage; and from our chosen standpoint we can regard both kinds of courage, or the deeds flowing from them, as acts of risking one's own safety for someone else's sake or for the sake of a cause.

We can extend our main conception by giving unselfishness the meaning of self-sacrifice in the sense of giving away all one's goods, as Francis of Assisi is reported to have done, or one's own life, as many religious martyrs have. It may also be magnified into spiritual self-extinction, that is, one's own complete immersion in the universe, as Buddhist saints are believed to do, or try to do. In this case unselfishness is primarily that of a state of mind, and the action, related to it, fasting or solitude coupled with contemplation are secondary.

So, if we ask 'What is the good?' the answer is that the good is circumscribed by a 'system of ideas' built up in the manner shown. Further it has become clear that the good, which cannot be defined in the usual way—that is, by two terms—may be delineated as explained, though neither definitively (the system remains capable of progression) nor absolutely. As to progression, the system is

[1] Aristotle, *Nicomachean Ethics* v, 1 and 3.

able to grow indefinitely both in richness and in firmness through the introduction of further notions of ethical relevance and the application of our central conception to them. It is not absolute because the choice of a central conception remains open to continuing reflection.

In a sense, our attempt to circumscribe the good was meant rather as a way of showing how a notion may be *developed systematically* than as a contribution to moral philosophy. Such a contribution, if it is within my power to make one, will be found in the second part of this treatise and, as already indicated, it will centre on the notion, not of the 'good', but the 'better'.

(b) After Moore, moral philosophy in England proceeded on logical-positivist and linguistic lines. Both these approaches, however, though they lead to different conclusions, have two points in common: value is a central concept to them, and they reduce the various values to one basic and all-embracing value, Moore's 'good'. The conclusions reached by the logical positivists on ethics have been stated with oft-commended clarity by A. J. Ayer.[1] Ayer distinguishes two principal classes of propositions relating to ethics: (1) Propositions analysing ethical concepts; (2) (a) empirical statements concerning behaviour, and (b) exhortations to be virtuous, often followed by (c) judgements on questions of vice or virtue. He proceeds to demonstrate at some length that all empirical statements and all judgements as such are subjective; they merely express what one or another individual believes is morally right or should be done and, if done, constitutes a valuable action to have been performed. He dismisses moral exhortations as merely edifying talk. Hence, he continues, all such propositions spring from accidental experiences or idiosyncratic reactions to particular experiences of individuals. It follows that no universally valid rule can be established on such a basis. Neither exhortations nor moral judgements, Ayer concludes, can be part of philosophy in the proper sense of that term, and therefore all that remains for a philosopher to do is logically to analyse ethical concepts with as much stringency as he is capable of applying. This conclusion obviously transforms ethics into little more than a field of exercise or practice-ground for logicians, and one is almost inclined to compare this exploitation of ethical problems with the use made of them in the ancient Roman

[1] *Language, Truth and Logic*, ch. 6.

schools of rhetoric.

The logical positivists' conclusion on moral philosophy, as stated by Ayer, has come to be accepted as *the* characteristic modern variant of moral scepticism. For, as Ayer states, all propositions based on value-judgements are non-normative, subjective and in no sense of universal validity; they are 'emotive'.[1]

In the context of such mere logical treatment of ethical problems, Moore's criticism of what he called the 'naturalistic fallacy' has played an important part. Generally speaking, responsibility for this fallacy has been attributed to those who make value-judgements without awareness of the fact that such judgements are merely emotive and non-philosophical. More important, and in purely logical terms, the fallacy has been ascribed to philosophers who fail to see that no 'ought'-proposition can logically be derived from an 'is'-proposition; that is, that when someone judges that an objective or aim is *good* it does not follow that he or others are compelled to pursue or achieve this aim.

As we have seen, the error of deriving an 'ought' from an 'is' was first pointed out by Hume. But the point that Hume wished to make was altogether different from the conclusions reached by the modern philosophers (except perhaps Moore). Hume does not deny morality as such, that is, the possibility of distinguishing objectively between moral and immoral actions. All Hume wished to convey was that the desire to achieve something good or bad was prior to any intellectual act of discerning between good and bad, value and non-value. Hume held further that, when a desire to act existed, reason was brought in subsequently in order to subject this desire or its aim to its own scrutiny and to decide on its relative or absolute worth. Logical-positivist philosophers, on the other hand, are radical sceptics. In stressing that no 'ought' must be derived from an 'is' their purpose is to demonstrate the merely subjective nature of any 'ought', because in their view only 'is'-propositions are objective in character (ie. capable of being verified or falsified, as the case may be, by factual observation).

(c) More recently the English moral philosophers, among whom Urmson and Hare appear to be the most eminent, have discussed

---

[1] The word 'emotive', which was introduced by Ogden and Richards in *The Meaning of Meaning*, characterizes Ayer's rejection of value judgements. (Cf. M. Warnock, *Ethics Since 1900*, 3rd ed., Oxford 1978.)

moral values or the 'good' on linguistic rather than logical-positivist lines.[1]

Urmson has expressed the view that since values constitute the essential factor of ethics all moral theories depend on how values are graded; or, methodically speaking, on what criteria of grading are employed for them.[2] To discover these criteria, Urmson believes, language holds the key, and so, after analyzing the all-embracing term for value—that is, the *good*—he comes to the conclusion that the criteria of values, and any particular moral code derived from these criteria, emanate either from an authoritative source such as the government, or, not from society as a whole, but from social groups within the overall society. And with this, as each society encompasses many social groups, Urmson is able to explain why within one society the grading criteria and moral codes differ. He can also explain why, even where the grading and the criteria are agreed within one group of people, individuals of the group may still differ in their views on particular cases, because such views depend not exclusively on general principles but on specific judgements.

As one reflects on Urmson's moral theory three aspects stand out. It is built on sociological foundations; it makes the standards not of society as a whole but of societies within society the sources of moral codes; and it uses the methods of linguistics to discover the values of such groups.

Considering not only Urmson's views but those of others who think on similar lines, it is clear that all sociological-linguistic ethics are a variant, not of ethical scepticism, but of relativism. For, depending on the time or place of a person's life, his moral code will differ from the moral codes of others, and yet be fully valid for him as a member of his social group within an overall society.

---

[1] Nowell-Smith in his *Ethics* (1954) uses the linguistic method to demonstrate the validity of the logical-positivist position. In a sense, he started where Ayer had left off or, rather, produced that ethics which Ayer had postulated. Nowell-Smith analyzes words and their uses and concludes that there are three classes of words: A-words, which are apt to arouse emotions; G-words which are imperatives (gerundiva) and D-words which are purely descriptive. One of the points he makes is that the usual syntactical way of classifying words does not stand up to philosophical scrutiny. For example, a word which appears to be descriptive like 'praiseworthy' is in fact not a D-word but a G-word, namely a command to do the praiseworthy thing.

[2] 'On grading', *Mind* vol. 59, pp. 145ff.

(d) R. M. Hare, probably the most original of the English moral philosophers since Moore, not only combines linguistics with mathematical logic for his method but also, as regards his matter, synthesises continental thinking, especially on the importance of personality, with that of the ethical positivists in England who are guided by sociological views. In his first book he shows himself still wholly concerned with linguistic analyses of moral propositions and concepts. But in his second book, *Freedom and Reason* (1965)—followed by several articles defending it[1]—he strikes a new note.

Hare's ethics is founded on two main principles. First, there is the principle that it must be possible for a moral command to be expressed as a generally applicable proposition if that command is to be a valid rule. That is to say, according to Hare, whatever criteria of value and consequently rule of conduct an individual may choose to adopt, such a rule cannot be called a philosophical norm unless it is conceived as universally valid. Secondly, every individual, Hare holds, is free to choose his own criteria of value and value-grading, and consequently his own values. It might seem to follow from (1) and (2) that all ethical commands emanate from individuals and so, paradoxically, that the particular is equal to the universal, or that relative is absolute. But this is by no means Hare's teaching. For it is clear that Hare's theory is to be understood in formal, logical, terms, and that his principles have no specific application to any given contents. For all Hare wants to say is that formally speaking no rule can be a *rule* unless it is 'universalizable', and that, if it is not, whether or not it is morally acceptable, it is not a rule.

Indeed, Hare is at pains to correct any wrong conclusion that might be drawn from what he says about his two principles and especially the conclusion that whatever an individual conceives of as a 'universalizable' rule is a valid ethical maxim. Hare's individual is not a legislator. For, Hare points out, if he were, he might propagate a thoroughly bad rule, overcoming resistance to it by distorting facts. Consequently, to avert this possibility and in the true positivist tradition, Hare stresses the importance of ascertaining facts; of clearly distinguishing between factual and value judgements. Here follows a quotation from Hare's *Freedom and Reason*:

There are fanatics who by concealing facts and arousing passions

[1] *Essays on the Moral Concepts*, London 1972.

will cloud the sympathetic imagination—in short by all the familiar methods of propaganda. These methods would have less power over people if one essential condition for their success were removed: confused thinking . . . If a person is able to distinguish genuine facts from those 'facts' which are really concealed evaluations; if in short he is clear-headed enough to stick to the moral question that he is asking . . . then the propagandists will have little power over him. To arm people in this way against propaganda is the function of moral philosophy.[1]

Undoubtedly, Hare's insistence that any rule which is a valid rule must have universal application owes much to his study of symbolic logic, and in particular to the role which the quantifier plays in it. But there is also some resemblance to be noted between his views and Kant's: like Kant, Hare has designed a formalist ethics, and like Kant he makes his command a universally applicable one.

On the other hand Hare's views bear some similarity to those of Kierkegaard, Nietzsche and the existentialists. For, like Kierkegaard and the others mentioned, Hare gives the individual conceived of as personality unlimited freedom to choose his values or decide what is good or bad. In short, Hare's philosophy as developed in *Freedom and Reason* is logical formalism applied to personality ethics.

I have concentrated so far on *Freedom and Reason*, Hare's second book, for which he himself regarded his first as preparatory. In that book he had devoted much attention to language and, in particular, to distinguishing between descriptive and prescriptive statements, mainly for the purpose of clarifying the term 'emotive' in its relation to 'value'. Hare has further enriched linguistic thinking both in his second book and in the articles he wrote after that book's publication in defence of its main tenets. For there Hare attempts to prove that any universalized principle of a person's moral preference or choice comes alive in language, or may even be tied to the mode of language which he uses either as a unique individual or as a member of a social group, and hence that the moral preferences of groups and persons can be discovered through analyses of their vocabulary, grammar, style—in short, usage of language. Here Hare once again reveals that his approach to moral

[1] *Freedom and Reason*, p. 185.

philosophy, no matter what method he uses, is not rigidly bound either to sociological or individualistic doctrines or to positivist-sceptical conclusions, but is designed to be comprehensive— encompassing the entire spectrum of ethical thinking.

PART TWO
Outline of a Theory of Ethics

Introduction

As so much thought has been devoted to ethics since antiquity it would be impossible to devise any ethical philosophy independently of previous thinking. However, it does not follow that there can be no new ethical theory which is not an eclectic mosaic of views already expressed. The ethics offered here, though rooted in earlier philosophy, is designed to be unitary. Its purpose is, to be useful, at least in the circumstances of the present. I do not intend to discuss the metaphysics of ethics, whether in a theistic or a humanistic sense—that is, I make no attempt to search for the 'ultimate' source of the moral command whether it is derived from the divine will or from human reason. Rather, the ethics offered is based on observation such as we can carry out on ourselves as individuals—as fellows of other individuals, as members of a society—on other individuals, and finally on society as such. It does, however, seek corroboration in the views of some of the eminent moral philosophers of the past; and it is presented in the form of three theses, each followed by comment, consisting of explanations and defence.

However, before proceeding to these theses, we shall have to clarify a preliminary question: namely, What is the area of ethics? In recent tradition ethics is conceived as concerned with private virtues or the conduct of private individuals towards each other. Hence it is bounded on the one side by the restrictions imposed by the laws of a country and on the other by a line excluding the morally irrelevant. It follows that (1) ethics relates to that middle area of human conduct which is not subject to the constraint of the law and in which, therefore, men are free to act or to refuse to act without compulsion or the fear of retribution by the power of the state. Crime therefore can have no place in ethical discussions, because (a) to commit a crime is held to be indisputably immoral, and (b) it is the responsibility of the state to deal with it. In other words ethics is not concerned with abnormally evil actions or attitudes; its enquiries and rules relate to the actions of ordinary men and women, that is, to the large majority of people. As to (2), it is easy to point out decisions or inclinations which are ethically irrelevant—for example, whether one prefers holidaying by the sea or inland, or whether one prefers growing roses or carnations.

However, though in recent times ethics has frequently been treated as a subject on its own—and in particular as distinct from politics—ethics and politics are in fact closely interrelated: not only do they frequently overlap but they are essentially bound up with each other. Again and again people are found to have such strong and fervent moral convictions that they combine to form groups for the explicit purpose of exerting pressure on their governments—sometimes to ban and sometimes to establish certain practices—for example, to prohibit pornographic literature, or to legitimize divorce and second marriages in church. In short, ethical reformers throughout the ages have attempted, often successfully, to influence decisions made by the state; or even to alter the structure of a state's organs and institutions and its very constitution, defying existing laws. Indeed, the more deeply one reflects on their relationship the more clearly it emerges that ethics without politics is unavailing, and politics without ethics is bound to fail in the end.

A. First Thesis

Man, who is primarily motivated by the impulse of self-preservation, is also, and with comparable force, motivated by an impulse to be helpful, good-neighbourly; nor is there any conflict between these two motivations, because not only the first but also the second is natural.

COMMENT. What is man? Man is myself and yourself viewed as members of a species sharing with most other members of the same species these same basic characteristics: the impulse to self-preservation, or rather the impulse to maintain and increase one's power to protect oneself (Hobbes), and a second impulse, to be helpful to others, which has been called 'benevolence' by Cumberland, a term which is used in this sense also by Hume. 'Benevolence' as a term is preferable to Comte's 'altruism', because altruism implies a conflict within ourselves, between our impulse of self-preservation and inclination to help others. The doctrine of conflict presupposes dualistic view of man—that is, the view that ethical action is dictated to man by a power outside his nature, whether that power be called God or practical reason, and that man left to his own natural impulses is animal-like, brutish, instinctively preying on others and working for himself alone. But this is not the case. Even casual observation shows that it is within man's nature to be good to himself and good to others, and that we do not have to conquer our own selfishness each time to exercise benevolence. Indeed there are people who fight as vigorously for their right to be charitable as others do in the furtherance of their own interests.

However, though one need not speak of conflicts, overlaps do occur. We are often faced with dilemmas due not to our own divergent inclinations but to a situation in which we find ourselves. It is in such situations that judgement and character each have a role to play.

The following is meant by 'overlap': it frequently, if not continually, happens that individuals have to weigh up which of two or more demands should come first, that is, which course of action they should take, whether in their own interest or in the exercise of some duty as they conceive it. In some cases therefore an individual will ask himself which claim is more pressing, that of his own direct interest or that of someone else's needs. His decision on an issue of this kind will be made by his faculty of judgement. Yet his choice may not be solely a rational one: an individual's character, even his upbringing, the circumstances of his life, and so on, will play their part in the decision. For instance, there may be a conflict of loyalties within him. Or a person of an excessively selfish character in a particular situation will always put his own interest, however slight, before someone else's needs though these may be very great. In most cases self-interest will be served before benevolence comes into play. Besides there are occasions when an individual is not sure that his own security is fully guaranteed, while nevertheless a demand is made on his benevolence. In such cases, once again, character is of prime importance. A person's decision, whether he should follow the impulse of selfishness or that of benevolence, or indeed even risk his security to exercise kindness, does not depend on human nature in general but on a particular individual's qualities—his generosity or meanness, his courage or lack of it, and so on.

It may even be objected that there are people who, far from being actuated by a desire to be good, are in fact driven by impulses of cruelty or sadism, either because they are embittered by previous experiences or because they are sexually perverted. It is possible to reply to this objection that even such people—unfortunate people perhaps—nevertheless on some occasions act kindly either towards *some* human beings or towards animals. But the main answer to this criticism must be that, though people exist who are motivated by hatred, or who even enjoy being harsh and malicious, the majority of us are naturally inclined to be good to others, not of course to everybody they know but, and this is the important fact, to those they casually meet and find in need of help, and *a fortiori* to those liked or loved by them. That is to say, the realization that there are malevolent people does not invalidate the thesis that benevolence is part of human nature as such. In short, when a person is faced with the choice between two or more possibilities of action, the decision must not be conceived as the result of a struggle between selfishness and good will within him, because both these impulses are within his nature, but as a matter to be decided in each case on its merits and demerits, that is, in the same way as if it were a choice between two or more contrasting possibilities of serving a selfish interest, which comprises one's own and someone else's.

B. Second Thesis

Since an individual's life is a continuous battle in which he tries to maintain or increase his power of self-preservation, the rules of ethics must relate to this battle; and since man is willing to consider others beside himself, they must relate to it in such a manner as to mitigate, civilize and humanize it. In other words, the precepts of ethics should be understood not so much as rules as peace as of war.

COMMENT. The struggle of life is fought on two fronts: man wages it both against the forces of nature and against his fellows. In the first sense of the word our struggle is with objects, adverse circumstances, and so on. In the second sense we compete with our fellow-men for food, clothing, shelter and, beyond these essentials, luxuries. Often we are engaged in an actual physical or mental fight against opponents or a particular adversary whose success, or even life, may mean our own failure, misfortune and sometimes death. In short, there is no action, or even thought directed towards action, which cannot be conceived of as a fight, that is, a bracing of oneself against obstacles or—more important within the context of a moral study—against one's fellow-men. There are degrees of force or intensity with which the struggle may be conducted. Moreover what is permitted either by the law or outside the law—that is, morally—is subject to wide variations, depending on time and place. Still, the basic moral principle remains the same. None of the forms of the struggle is blameworthy in itself, because not only in its mildest but also in its fiercest degree the battle is natural so long as it flows from our impulse to self-preservation. For example, against mortal danger any kind of self-defence is permitted, both legally and morally. And so, in whatever shape or to whatever degree the struggle is fought, one rule applies, namely, to humanize it to the extent to which this can be achieved at any given time.

One may ask: Why is it that men cannot live in harmony together but always have to struggle against each other? I cannot attempt to answer this question. Perhaps experimental psychology has the answer.[1] Or perhaps the following simple explanation suffices, that the need of the inhabitants of the earth is greater than the supplies which the earth provides. We can only say that the struggle is natural and that man, either because of his character as such or because certain qualities are forced upon him, has a strong militant trait. Indeed it appears that man needs adversaries, either because he habitually feels threatened and is convinced that 'anticipation', a pre-emptive strike, is the best defence (cf. Hobbes), or because he needs an adversary as a spur to his energy, in whatever field. One may go even so far as to say that man 'sets' adversaries; that is, he decides whether consciously or subconsciously that someone, a man or a woman, is his adversary whom he must struggle against, or at least not lose sight of, as he works or acts or plans. In brief, if we have no adversary *we create one*.

On the other hand, we not only deal with opponents, we also have allies. To look for allies is as natural for us as to seek

---

[1] There are of course also psychoanalytical explanations, e.g. those connecting this general trait of human nature with a person's early relationship to his father or mother, or even his growth in the womb.

adversaries; these two notions—of 'opponents' and 'allies'—are interrelated. Therefore, to say that man is engaged in a life-long struggle is the same as to say that he is continually dealing both with adversaries and with allies.

It should be added that adversaries can cease to be adversaries or even turn into allies and vice versa; and also, importantly enough, that there may be, or normally will be, an element of struggle even between allies; that is, that the relationship with one's allies is hardly ever a relationship of simple co-operation but one in which an element of competition or struggle is nearly always inherent.

After discussing what is meant by 'struggle', we turn to the question of the rule. Principally, the rule is designed either to outlaw certain practices employed in the struggle or to moderate them.

So there is only one basic rule, but it must not be rigidly stated; its wording is to be free. It is not to be expressed as one formula but can be stated in many and various ways, or even tentatively, so that it fits different conditions and remains adjustable as times and circumstances change. Here follow some examples of how the basic rule may be expressed. 'Do not inflict more hardship on anyone, including yourself, than your own safety or basic needs require.' 'Although you will regard some people as your opponents, never regard them as your enemies.' 'Always consider what your action will mean to others before you decide on it.' And so on.

For as indicated before, the essential concept of ethics is not the 'good' but the 'better'. However we must clarify what is meant by 'the better': it does not mean drawing nearer to perfection but only drawing away from the bad, in a dual way: by maintaining what has been achieved while times, and with the times the manifestations of evil, change; and also progressively, as our awareness of the problems of morals and their possible solution grows.

Whereas it is obvious that the Second Thesis of this treatise owes a great deal to at least two sixteenth-century thinkers, Hobbes and Grotius, it is perhaps not quite so apparent that it is indebted also to Kant. Hobbes saw self-preservation, and with it the desire to acquire power for the purpose of self-preservation, as the primary motive of all human action. But whereas Hobbes proceeds from his first assumption to explain the founding of organized communities under sovereign princes, under our thesis private ethics and politics are treated as continually and permanently interrelated. The manner in which this treatise is indebted to Grotius can be expressed in somewhat similar terms. What we owe to Grotius is his new doctrine that even in war certain rules—which he derives from 'Natural Law'—should be observed; in other words, that not even in war is everything to be considered permissible, but certain actions should be banned, such as offences against common humanity, acts of atrocity and so on. Now, whereas Grotius is concerned with politics—that is, with wars between nations or civil wars—our Second Thesis is designed to adapt the rules designed by Grotius to the conflicts of private life. In other words, reversing Grotius' and to some extent Hobbes's approach, political rules are here reinterpreted in ethical terms and, instead of applying moral rules to politics, we try to derive from political life such maxims as will provide *moral philosophy with an achievable objective*.

Finally, comparing the rule here proposed with Kant's teaching, our thesis shares with Kant's imperative the conviction that there can be only one moral rule and that this rule must be universally valid. It is, however, a weakness of the categorical imperative that it is stated as a single formula and that Kant considers this formula to be valid at all times, past, present and future, and thereby makes it rigid, that is, independent of changing circumstances, varying societies, and so on. But while guidance by one rule must remain the foundation of all ethical teaching, that rule should be capable of being stated in many ways and thus, in any particular conditions, adjusted to these conditions. And once it has been so adjusted it should be expressed as powerfully and strikingly as can be by those who are professionally engaged in moral teaching or elect themselves as committed to such teaching, because they believe that they are capable of it on account of their eloquence or through their charismatic appeal to the rest of us.

C. Sociology and Ethics

Sociology is a comparatively recent discipline. Its founding father, so to speak, was Max Weber, a Heidelberg professor, who in a famous book[1] investigated the relationship between Protestantism

[1] Max Weber, *The Protestant Ethic and the Spirit of Capitalism*, London 1930. The German original of this work appeared in Tuebingen in 1904-5.

and early Capitalism, a connection which he had discovered. After the success of this book he proceeded to study group beliefs and attitudes, the functioning of authority in national communities, or sections of them, as well as the impact of Hinduism and Buddhism on norms of behaviour, aims, actions and so on.

Weber, who belonged to the pre-1914 generation, did not believe that it was possible to present a true picture of human actions solely on the basis of causal explanations. Hence he divided his attention between mechanically, or causally, created reality and ideas, or rather he investigated the interplay of ideas and factual reality. This is clearly visible in his study of authority. Weber distinguishes four categories of organization over which authority functions each time in a different manner: (1) a group or tribe following a 'charismatic' leader; (2) a feudal society obeying its feudal overlord; (3) a bureaucracy serving a central government whether monarchical or republican; (4) a modern professional organization bound by its own laws. To each of these organized groups, or the authority enjoyed over them, Weber ascribed legitimacy, but a different kind of legitimacy in each instance and each with its own criterion. He called the criterion 'truth', by which he meant not absolute truth but the general belief on which obedience in those various instances is based, namely, charisma, feudal sovereignty, firmly established central government, professional self-esteem and mutual respect arising from skill and training.

Influenced, too, by the high regard in which personality was held in his time, Weber stressed the subjective component of attitudes, behaviour and especially valuations. He conceded that the ideas valid at a time, the totality of which he called *Kultur*, was of paramount importance to every individual, but in the last analysis, according to Weber, each individual, by interpreting the *Kultur* of his time from the fulness of his own personality, arrives at his own valuation and—as Weber adds, in harmony with the spirit of his time—it is those personal valuations which give meaning to each person's own existence in this world.

By contrast Karl Mannheim (also a Heidelberg professor), who wrote his main work[1] in the twenties, set out rigorously to exclude 'ideology' from all sociological research. It has to be added, however, that whereas in normal usage the term 'ideology' includes

[1] Karl Mannheim, *Ideologie und Utopie*, Heidelberg 1929 (London 1936); *Systematic Sociology*, London 1957.

visionary or utopian thought Mannheim, narrowing its meaning, used it merely to signify the intellectual superstructure which authority employs to maintain its control over those governed by it; while on the other hand he assigned the term 'utopian' to the notions and doctrines of those opposed to an existing order, and hence concluded that utopian thought was as much derived from reality as 'ideology', but negatively, in the sense that it fastens on those aspects of a social order which the 'utopian' rebels wish removed. In criticizing all previous social thinkers Mannheim believed that the preoccupation of his predecessors with ideals and principles had obscured and even distorted the study of reality, and he therefore made it his task to investigate social structures in what one may call a 'positivist' way. Thus sociology in the full modern sense of the word was born, as basically an empirical science exploring the world of human affairs in its fulness with all its innumerable and indeed infinite variations. The relations of the larger communities to the smaller within them, of groups to other groups, of groups to individuals, of types of individuals to other types of them, and so on, were to be, and since have been, abundantly studied. And naturally, in connection with such enquiries, the forces that function within societies, such as social control, customs, as well as the manner in which customs influence attitudes, kinds of behaviour and so on have been investigated also. In short, sociology was to be an all-embracing science extending from habits, traditions, law, economics and governmental authority to the psychology of the individual.

Looking back, it is easy to see that sociology as it was conceived by Karl Mannheim in the twenties constituted an almost inevitable reaction to the value theories of the then dominant transcendental and phenomenological schools. For it is characteristic of both those schools that they attempted to discover, or indeed professed to have found, permanent, universal, *a priori* values. They further believed that they were able to establish permanently valid scales of values and, strangely enough, such values as the admiration of beauty, true love and so on were placed high on the scale. Patently, ideas previously formed and already held with conviction were sought and 'uncovered' by those thinkers in the reality of life. Therefore, in opposition to such approaches, purely empirical investigations of reality as undertaken by Karl Mannheim and his followers were a necessary consequence; and this all the more so, because positivist enquiries were as much considered to be part of exact research, both in the natural sciences and the humanities, as was the study of ideas and their history.

To be consistent, sociology must at best be morally neutral. Mannheim himself—though after he had settled in England, he moved from his early, disinterested, Heidelberg approach to sociology as a pure research scientist to a greater appreciation of the merits of practical social reform—never abandoned his total rejection of the view that abstract principles or pure ideas are factors contributing to social stability or change. He explained structural changes of society largely as the results of new inventions leading not only to economic reorganization but also to bureaucratic reforms. These in turn entail novel methods of training members of the community, who thereby acquire a new status within society. Similarly he explained the existing state of affairs as stemming from previous more or less mechanical innovations. 'Customs which build up to a social order are equal to a moral order,' he taught.[1]

Since Mannheim's time a large literature covering general and specific aspects of human relations and interrelations has accumulated, which follows Mannheim's teaching but accentuates his basic position, namely, that all social concepts depend on, and are derived from, existing social conditions. As a result sociology has grown to be not only relativistic but in effect morally destructive.

Sociologists and non-sociologists will agree that there is nothing that exercises a greater influence on the attitudes and actions of individuals than a prevailing 'climate of opinion', which I shall call 'Opinion' for short.

The term 'climate of opinion' is deliberately chosen. It should not be confused with 'public opinion', which means opinions as expressed in the newspapers and so on, with reference to a particular event or situation and at a particular moment. A 'climate of opinion', on the other hand, covers a vast variety, though perhaps not the totality, of issues which are either under debate in a country or are simply accepted at any given time and place. Climate of opinion, or Opinion, is also preferable to such terms as 'society' or 'society opinion' (terms chosen by J. S. Mill) because 'society' is often used in a limiting sense. For since, historically, the term is

[1] *Systematic Sociology*, p. 127.

derived from high society, it usually refers to an exclusive circle of people, an élite whether aristocratic or intellectual. Similarly the term culture (*Kultur*) is unsuitable, because it also refers to an élite and moreover applies to Western countries only. Nor is *Weltanschauung* appropriate, because it is essentially connected with individuals as an attribute of personality.

Opinion comprises general and specific judgements, approvals and condemnations, valuations, their gradings and their criteria, for example the relative esteem in which birth, honours, money, titles, public position are held. Or, Opinion consists of the views, some primary, some subsidiary, shared by a large majority of the people among whom you live, that is, everyone, barring a few eccentrics. Such views are firmly maintained on most issues. Some however are allowed to be open to debate; and it may be said, without sophistry, that the very concession of freedom of debate on selective issues is also part of prevailing Opinion. For instance, in modern democracies many political, religious or cultural questions, though by no means all, may be discussed in public; whereas in fascist or communist countries many of the same issues, even cultural ones, are banned from debate.

In the Middle Ages Opinion was disseminated by priests, by itinerary monks and by travellers in general. Nowadays it is spread by the newspapers and television—the so-called 'mass-media'. These, of course, are mainly directed either by the authorities or by societies within society, and so to a large extent was the spread of news in former ages.

D. *Third Thesis*

Opinion is not the source of moral precepts; on the contrary, it is the object or target of ethical thought.

COMMENT. As we have seen, the sociologists deny the impact of what they call 'abstract principles' on social conditions and their changes. Their outlook is deterministic, almost fatalistic. According to them, social structure is brought about by causes, whether necessary or coincidental, which one may well describe as materialistic. 'Ideas', on the other hand, they hold, are evolved through pure conceptual reasoning, divorced from reality, their purpose being either to support an existing order or to attack some selected aspects of it. In more than one sense, the sociological approach is modelled on that of Marxism, and characteristically Mannheim's critique of Marxism is directed against the pre-dominance of *one* doctrine in it, namely, that of the class struggle. Instead Mannheim lists several other equally strong influences on individuals *qua* members of society—for instance, religion, patriotism, nationalism, party allegiances. To what lengths Mannheim is prepared to go to exclude 'abstract ideas' from sociological theory is apparent from his doctrine of types of behaviour. Group norms, he says, are not abstract rules but patterns of attitudes modelled on the conduct of some admired or revered person, whether that person is alive or belongs to the past.[1]

Clearly, the sociologists do not make unity or consistency their aim. Their objective is to observe and record reality which, they say, is not only infinitely varied but a most complex mixture of forces, circumstances, motives and causes and, viewed as a whole, a web the various strands of which they do not claim to be able to disentangle.

It is hardly necessary to point out that in maintaining their inflexible denial of the role which 'abstract ideas' play in the moulding of society the sociologists commit the error of confusing pure, speculative, thought with thought as such and, in the area of ethics, with reflections aimed at practical progress.

Thought of this latter kind is capable of making an impact on Opinion, and if it is to exercise a moral influence it must aim at mitigating the manner in which the battle of life is fought. It follows that in the face of a prevailing Opinion it is the task of the moral philosopher to point out *excesses* likely to emanate from it. This he can do by arguing, for example by indicating the evil to which such excesses may lead. He can also attempt to extend the area of actions to be frowned upon, i.e. of that which is 'not done', so long as such extension is aimed not at acerbation but moderation. In other words, the first guideline for the moral philosopher is: to point out excesses, thereby extending the sphere of actions to be avoided or criticized. As we shall see, his two main methods are (1) analysis, and (2) the constructive formation of alternatives to those aspects of Opinion which he considers harmful.

[1] Ibid., p. 11.

Opinion may be described as a *medium*, because only through penetrating Opinion can ethical instruction reach the minds, and influence the actions, of a large majority of individuals.

Many moral philosophers of the past have made one of the following two mistakes: some have ignored Opinion, addressing themselves directly to the individual; others have regarded Opinion as the ultimate source of morality. Among the first are most of the classical philosophers, including Kant; among the latter are those who teach that no universally valid ethics is possible. Other thinkers have tried to derive an ethics of material values from a prevailing Opinion and have even gone so far as to describe the values which ranked high in their own time and society as *a priori* and permanent. To avoid these two mistakes one has to steer a middle course, that is, neither ignore Opinion nor derive moral rules from it.

Still, even though Opinion is conceived as a medium, the rule which is to be applied to it is one of universal validity, and hence, because it is seen as universally applicable, it can be called 'formal'. For in itself the rule contains nothing material, and it acquires material content only by being applied to a specific situation. In this way therefore it is as formal as Kant's imperative, and indeed, since formalism is the only safeguard against ethical illusion arising from one's attachment to certain views prevailing at a particular time, only a formal rule is ethically sound. However, in contrast to Kant's imperative, the maxim here proposed is not assumed to be *a priori*, or pure, in the sense that some part of man's nature is excluded from its origin. On the contrary, as Hume points out, 'good will' is part of human nature; and since therefore the gratification of impulses inherent in nature may well lead to the avoidance of excesses of one kind or another, the rule suggested here does not conflict with the nature of man seen as a unitary whole.

From another viewpoint the precept to argue against excesses is compatible with the teaching of Aristotelian ethics, which emphasizes the mean. However, whereas Aristotle recommends the mean, i.e. the moderate disposition, as the right state of mind of the individual,[1] our rule concerning excess refers to conduct, and in particular conduct in the struggle of life; and in this respect our rule is related less to Aristotle's principle than to Grotius'.

Analogously, the moral philosopher should argue against excesses

[1] *Nicomachean Ethics;* see, e.g., II, 8.

arising from Opinion. Here follow two examples. At a time when Opinion was dominated by Darwin's theory of the survival of the fittest and Nietzsche's vision of the Superman, pure selfishness was accepted as a necessary or even admirable attitude to adopt. In a poetic and popular form such theories are reflected in the simile of the 'hammer' and the 'anvil'. The hammer is seen (though not realistically) as growing ever stronger, whereas the anvil, weakening all the time, perishes in the end. But it is obvious that in the course of his life every individual must be sometimes hammer and sometimes anvil, and therefore to tell one's fellow-men 'You must either be a hammer and survive or an anvil and perish', that is, to speak of a choice, means whipping up one's natural desire to achieve one's objective to a frenzy of self-assertion. Or, Opinion can lead to excesses in an opposite sense, namely where self-sacrifice is immoderately admired, either generally as in the Middle Ages, or in some closed societies even today, and so in arguing against such excesses it should be pointed out that self-sacrifice is to be respected only if it is done for an objective and not for its own sake.

What is Opinion-forming society? It is (1) the individual setting himself up as a judge of people's attitudes, views, tastes, habits, status; (2) the individual consulting with other individuals on judgements, general or particular, to be reached; (3) the individual becoming aware of judgements formed, and accepting them, those who do not being 'eccentrics'.

Changes of Opinion occur both before and after changes in social structure. In the latter case the change may be due to mechanical causes, for example, inventions, as the sociologists maintain; in the former, to cultural developments, such as religious or educational reforms, or the success of the realistic drama towards the end of the nineteenth century; even to subtle changes of moods and tastes, the staleness of old customs or the desire for something new. And no doubt ethical precepts may also contribute to changes of Opinion. Often such changes are widely publicized; frequently they creep in almost imperceptibly. Some are restricted and slow, others sudden and wide-ranging.

An example of a radical change of Opinion is provided by a comparison between the periods before 1914 and after 1918. Much of what had been held inviolate and sacred was treated with indifference or contempt in the decade which followed the end of the First World War. Many former beliefs, traditions, valuations were abandoned; new values were set up. A special instance of altered views can be found in the contrast between the harsh anti-abortion, anti-divorce, anti-adultery views, and laws, of the earlier time and the freedom or even licentiousness in sexual matters to which we have now become generally accustomed.

While any member of the public may react both sentimentally and intellectually to such facets of Opinion as offend him, the special tasks of the moral philosopher are (1) to analyze Opinion, or certain of its aspects and (2), if he feels that he is able to, to form constructive new ideas to replace those of which he disapproves.

Analysis, as I understand the term, consists mainly in the reduction of Opinion or some of its facets not merely to their historical origin but to a central idea which permeates them. In the process of reduction, distortions of the original idea will frequently be discovered. Mysticism may serve as an example. Starting from the belief that what is impenetrable to reason is divine, the mystic attempts to identify himself with the Deity ecstatically, not in order to know the unknowable but to despise that which can be known. On another somewhat comparable example we have already touched: it is the transformation of religious worship into an equally fervent devotion to the values of secular culture, as occurred in the late nineteenth and early twentieth centuries. In some cases, philosophical clarification by itself through analysis and the reduction of a view to its true beginnings may be sufficient to bring about a change of opinion, namely, by alerting people to the errors or falsehoods to which they have fallen victim. Generally the uncovering of a purpose underlining some aspect of Opinion, and especially those aspects which are assiduously fostered by particular groups or their agents, may purge the minds of people in general and thereby exercise a strong influence on Opinion.

As to the second task of the philosopher, namely, to make attempts at producing constructive new ideas, it is easier to describe the method by which this can be done than to give examples. This follows from the very nature of the requirement. For we are in need of new views to supersede some of the bad existing ones, and as we long to receive them we have to wait for some inspired person to give them to us. Therefore the best one can do by way of illustration is to refer to the past and choose some historical example. That

6

famous triad of ideas, *liberté*, *égalité*, *fraternité*, the realization of which the men of the French Revolution proclaimed as their ultimate objective, may serve. Nowadays the words expressing those ideas may appear to be mere slogans or party cries, but in fact, and in their own time, they were not catch-words but doctrines. *Liberté* was directed against autocratic government, *égalité* against class distinctions and *fraternité* against racial discrimination. Let us concentrate on the last. *Fraternité* transfers the idea of brotherly fellowship from the family, the clan, the tribe, the nation, to all mankind. In its time the impact of that new notion of *fraternité* was immensely powerful. All human beings were created alike, it was held; all virtues were distributed equally among them (the 'noble savage'); relations between the races were uninhibited. Racial superciliousness would meet with astonishment, incredulity, reprobation. It was natural for anyone, following the Roman tradition, to associate with people of all races in service, office, friendship. In short, *fraternité* was a many-sided reality, as is proved by innumerable examples.[1] Today this is by no means so. And the reason for this change of Opinion is that none of those three ideas of 1789 has retained either its strength or its original meaning. *Liberté* has been confused with licentiousness, a society seeking equality is described as *egalitarian* and the concept on which we are concentrating, *fraternité*, is debased by the sectarian connotation it has acquired. Evidently *fraternité*, like *liberté* and *égalité*, is no longer useful in the context of present-day Opinion. Surely, however, if it was possible at one time to evolve ideas which had a powerful effect because they were inspiring and considered right by people, it should be possible once again to develop ideas of an ethical nature and make them useful by adapting them to existing Opinion.

Generally speaking, Opinion since the Renaissance can be characterized as reflecting, on the one hand, a desire for ever greater freedom and, on the other, the realization that the imposition of restrictions on freedom is a necessity of human life, or for a social order to be created and maintained. Correspondingly moral thought has generally been concerned in some instances with reducing and in other instances with extending such restrictions as have been in force at any particular time and place.

[1] One may say that this is also proved by the fierce reaction which the idea of *fraternité* provoked, and indeed first in France, as expressed in the writings of Count Gobineau.

At this point it is necessary for me to explain what is meant by thought. By thinking I understand an act aimed at generalizing a direct perception by transferring it to the idea of another direct perception, whether its object is internal or external, or to a thought based on direct perceptions. The products of such transference will be, first, an idea which is generally applicable to further direct perceptions, and secondly, if this original idea is consistently applied, a system of ideas, a *doctrine*. For this doctrine to be useful, the ideas of which it consists must be as closely as possible adapted to existing Opinion, or rather to as many as feasible of the facets of a prevailing Opinion.

Among the terms now used for thinking, it is difficult to find one appropriate for thought as I understand it. 'Concept' is linked to genus and species. 'Conception' may mean concept, interpretation, theory. 'Idea' stands for representation, theory and even utopian vision. Still, idea is useful in the sense of representation in general or representation of any kind. Notion is as ill-defined as thought itself: it may mean concept and it may also comprise much of what is implied in 'idea'. It appears necessary therefore to find a special term for thought as understood here.

Of the Greek words for thinking, *noein* seems to be the most adequate, because its meanings include 'to notice', 'to perceive' as well as 'to think'. From it the noun *noêsis*, which means the act of thinking, is derived. Now, since it is of the essence of thought that it conjoins two or more perceptions, the term *synnoêsis* seems to be the most suitable for the act of thinking and *synnoëma* for the object or content of the act or the idea arising from it.[1] If the aim is to form a consistent, comprehensive, theory, *one synnoëma*—the central *synnoëma*—has to be applied to as many relevant experiences as possible. When this is done a theory to be called *a synnoëtic system of ideas*—a tendency rather than a fixed doctrine—is born, the efficacy of which will evidently be all the greater (a) the more consistently and richly it is developed and (b) the more closely it is adapted to existing Opinion.

If once again we choose the historical idea of *fraternité* as our example, this time calling it a *central synnoëma*, its forcefulness will obviously depend on the subtlety with which it is adjusted to as

[1] Cf. my article 'Wahrheit und Methode' ('Truth and method') in *Zeitschrift fuer philosophische Forschung* 28, 2 (1974).

many aspects of life as possible, such as common religious beliefs, celebrations, education, entertainments and so on.

How can it be explained that overall, over the centuries, moral standards have improved, though certainly not continually but with many interruptions and reverses? This could not have happened if, in the course of time, the civilizing influence of thought and sentiment had not at some stages received the backing of powerful agencies, such as enthusiastic movements, religious or political, or the support of governments. Some of the changes brought about in this way were sudden and profound and hence widely noticed. However, slow and gradual developments which are hardly perceived as they occur should not be regarded as insignificant. For repeated criticism by philosophers and writers of excesses arising from prevailing Opinion may well produce in time an alteration of some generally held view.

Religion occupies a unique place in the history of moral progress. Its precepts, derived as they are from the belief in an omnipotent and omniscient God, maintained by great institutions, reinforced by the observance of a hallowed ritual, take deep roots in people, all the more so because they are taught to them from their earliest childhood. Therefore, these precepts are not easily forgotten; and in so far as they serve progress they are of inestimable value. The essence of religion, as opposed to superstition, is the belief in the ultimate triumph of good over evil or, in human terms, the expectation that benevolence in man will prove stronger not than selfishness but malevolence.

There are areas where the moral philosopher has no task, properly his own, to fulfil, and can offer no help.

To say that people are born with different characters is to state a commonplace truth. People are brave or cowardly, generous or mean, kind or hard-hearted; and, in accordance with such differences, lists of virtues and vices have been compiled. Now, because their characters vary some people are naturally inclined to be virtuous either in a general or in a particular sense of the word, whereas others are less so inclined. In other words, some people are very willing, others reluctant, to act in the way virtue—for example, generosity—demands. But not only their nature determines people's inclination; most of us are affected also by moods and by our physical state of health. A further complication is introduced by those who stress—as many do today—that each individual's qualities, his virtues or lack of them, are conditioned also by the social environments in which he grew up—by the love or lack of love he received from his parents. It follows that each individual presents his own problems. But since this is so, moral philosophy as such has no solution to offer. For example, if an Edwardian was inclined to be prodigal, incurring debts which were gravely injurious to his father or family, a moral philosopher would not have been better placed to dissuade him from pursuing his ways than, say, a parson, a physician or a friend, that is, some professional or non-professional adviser.

As to the virtues *in abstracto*, they have often been described, analyzed and graded. But although (I believe) there are some never-to-be-disputed-virtues, such as bravery or generosity, it is apparent that not only the grading of virtues but even their descriptions are based on varying conditions, on changing Opinion. In recent times some philosophers have expressed the view that the qualities we consider to be virtues are 'emotive', by which they mean that they are values based on *sentiments* arising from tradition, custom, class. Above all, however, no list of virtues can ever amount to an ethics, which is concerned not with specific qualities but with a universal rule. Of all moral philosophers only Aristotle has succeeded in transforming a catalogue of virtues into a system, namely by deciding on a distinguishing mark, the mean, which enabled him to define virtue as such, virtue in general.

Another problem, or rather two closely linked problems, namely, those of divided loyalty and conflicting duties, although they have often been the objects of ethical inquiry, are in fact outside the scope of the moral philosopher. It is apparent that each individual owes loyalty to several causes or persons—his country, religion, family, friends, employers, sometimes his party, even his club. Now, although each of these loyalties can be said to be justified or even commendable, it is clear that their grading as well as their description depends on circumstances—on where and when the individual lives. For instance, in Japan (I understand) loyalty to one's employers ranks higher than loyalty to one's family. In the pre-1914 era loyalty to one's country—patriotism—was regarded as the supreme duty, compared with which any other loyalty—to one's

Church, party, family and indeed one's own conscience—counted but nothing. Anyone who did not put his country first in an absolute sense risked death, or at the very least abject disgrace.[1] In our time, however, the duty of protecting one's own family from grave danger would be regarded as ranking at least equal with one's duty to fight in a foreign war. Furthermore, there are some politicians who openly state that they regard their duty to their party as being above their loyalty to the country. Other politicians have disputed such statements, from which it follows that the question of divided loyalty in this field is at present open to debate, and the same can certainly be said of many other dilemmas in this country as well as in other countries. Hence the moral philosopher, if he has any role at all to play in matters of this nature, can at most plead that party loyalty should not reach the degree of causing one's country ruin, or that loyalty to one's country should not be exercised to the point where it would bring about the destruction of one's party, which presumably is the champion of worthwhile principles or a great idea. In short, since the criteria of grading loyalties are changing continually, it would be wrong for a moral philosopher even to recommend, let alone attempt to impose, universally valid standards by which to assess the different kinds of loyalty. All he can do is to record what he observes generally and in individual cases, namely, that people who find themselves in a conflict of loyalties are swayed partly by their inclinations, preferences, moods but mainly by the majority view of the society to which they belong. Secondly, he may attempt to influence people not to become victims of extremism, by deprecating 'over-loyalty', say, to one's country, i.e. patriotism, which so easily degenerates into fanaticism. And thereby, as has been hinted at already and will be discussed further in the following section, a philosopher may gradually bring about the down-grading of a loyalty which he finds is too highly valued or, *vice versa*, cause the enhanced estimation of a loyalty which he believes is too little respected; and he will do so most effectively by inspiring a circle of people to create a movement designed to work towards that end.

Having dealt with divided loyalty, we have in a sense already discussed the question of conflicting duties—duties to one's employers, or an institution or one's family. There may be situations in a

---

[1] Whereas until after the Second World War it was unlawful for a soldier to disobey an order no matter what it entailed, now it is unlawful for him to execute an order if obedience involves him in committing an atrocity or crime.

person's life in which he is deeply troubled about which of two irreconcilable duties to fulfil, what course to follow, what action to take. For example, a person may doubt whether he should risk his career in public employment by refusing to go to his place of work or decline an urgent appeal from an ailing brother or friend to come and help him in a desperate situation. In cases like this judgment or common sense must decide; and naturally an individual's character will also play a significant part. The criterion which a person facing this kind of dilemma should use is the relative importance of the two causes he has to consider: the gravity of a friend's situation on the one hand and the risk of his own position and future career on the other.

This and similar cases are therefore not of a nature suited for a moral philosopher to intervene in. Rather they provide occasions for friends and advisers who might aid a person's own judgment, while the persons directly involved in situations as the one described can do no more than their best in accordance with their strength and judgment. And the old *Corpus Iuris* rule, too, is always applicable: *Ultra vires nemo obligatur*—no one can do more than his strength permits.

Another, purely theoretical, problem, that of determinism versus free will, has haunted moral philosophy for a long time. By determinism one understands the view that every one of a man's actions whether for good or bad is necessitated—determined by forces beyond his will, namely, his mental and physical capacities, his upbringing, his environment. It is clear from what has been said that the theory of determinism follows scientific lines and in particular the generally adopted view that all that happens, and especially all changes which occur in nature, constitute an unbroken chain of causes and effects. In the context of determinism man is seen as part of nature, both mentally and physically, and hence the conclusion is drawn that his decisions are not free but conditioned by causes working on his body or mind, or through his mind on his body and equally through his body on his mind. The theory of free will on the other hand implies that each person is free to choose how to act—wisely or unwisely, honestly or dishonestly, kindly or maliciously, in short, that he is able to choose either good or evil.

It follows for the adherents of determinism that nobody can be held responsible for his actions, not even for a crime he may commit, because all his actions are predetermined by forces beyond his control. Those who adopt this theory are often people calling themselves liberals and progressives, and no doubt determinism has been invoked for the furtherance of important and praise-worthy objectives, for instance, progressive prison reforms; whereas free will has been championed by conservatives, the Churches and, one may add, those who wish to defend the dignity of man. The inference seems to be that the two opposing sides, those who advocate determinism and those who uphold the theory of free will, are both motivated by extraneous intentions, and hence that the question of determinism versus free will has been introduced into moral philosophy for reasons which are heterogeneous to it, and that it may well be a question that forms no essential part of ethical inquiry. For if every action, good or bad, is necessitated by a cause or a chain of causes stretching far back, all influences—including religious precepts ingrained in most people from their childhood days, or someone's eloquent and touching pleading to do something good or kind, or an innate disposition to be friendly—all these are influences like any other influence or cause, compelling us to act in a certain way and no other. It is true, of course, that none of these causes can be stated as unambiguously as it is possible to state natural causes, for example, gravity. Personal inclinations, emotional reactions to persuasive pleading, beliefs and motivations change easily and are hard to grasp and to define. Or, as a linguistic philosopher might put it, two different language games have become intermingled and confused in the debate on determinism versus free will, namely, scientific language as suited, for example, for physics, and prescriptive language employed in the context of desires and appetites and designed to appeal to a person's sense of obligation or emotions.

In conclusion, unless one accepts Kant's doctrine, which presupposes that man is possessed of a dual nature and consists of an animal and a divine part; and that the animal part in us must always act selfishly and rapaciously without any consideration of objectives other than the fulfilment of its own (animal) desires and appetites; and that it is the divine component in human nature which, cutting across the ordinary chain of cause and effect, induces man to act morally against his own self-interest—unless, I say, one accepts this Kantian doctrine, there remains nothing to add to what has been explained before, namely, that the problem of determinism versus free will is an extraneous problem with regard to ethics and that, even if determinism is fully accepted without Kant's ingenious limitation (the impact of practical reason on the natural chain of causes and effects) the theory of determinism practically leaves everything as it is, that is, it can be integrated in ethical thinking without in the slightest degree modifying, let alone restructuring moral philosophy.[1]

E. Transition to Politics

That there exists a close mutual relationship between ethics and politics is evident; moreover it is abundantly proved by a study of the history of ethical thought from ancient times. Moral philosophers have tried to penetrate the sphere of politics, intent on transforming government, society, the constitution of states. In their turn politicians have often influenced moral views, mainly through the medium of Opinion, either by proclaiming a particular set of views as the official philosophy within their domain or by suppressing theories opposite to the philosophy they uphold.

We have distinguished before between gradual changes brought about by thought and its expression and rapid changes, seemingly complete reversals, of an existing state of affairs. In other words, whereas ethical appeals may slowly affect a nation's generally held views and, in consequence, its laws and customs—though the latter are usually transformed much later—great and decisive changes, as history proves, require the foundation of movements and the establishment of organizations and in the end can only be brought about by large-scale political action. Sometimes such action is started and completed within the boundaries of one country, but

---

[1] 'Now, when it is said by a fatalist that the whole constitution of Nature, that everything . . . is necessary and could not possibly have been otherwise, it is to be observed that this necessity does not exclude deliberation, choice, preference, and acting from certain principles and to certain ends . . .' Bishop Butler, *The Analogy of Religion*, pt. I, ch. 6. Incidentally, Butler's 'analogy' essentially means the philosophical equivalent to religion. Kant's 'analogies of experience' mean the transcendental counterparts of experience. Like the term postulate, the term analogy is understood by the eighteenth-century philosophers in a specific sense which quite significantly differs from its established, general, meaning.

often major changes occur under the influence of forces from abroad. It would of course be easy for us to exploit the present as a source of examples of Great Power influence on small countries. But by conjuring up a possible historical situation, which is linked to the present, we shall best be able to clarify the point to be made. If, say, an army under a general sent by a revolutionary government had reached India about two hundred years ago, the category of the 'untouchables' would have ceased to exist and no citizen of India living today would either regard himself or be regarded by others as 'untouchable'.

Whatever the circumstances may be, government has a powerful influence both on the shaping of Opinion and its transformation and on manners and habits. This is equally true in times of steady and continuous government as in periods following violent changes. A good example of the latter is the alteration of Opinion resulting from the replacement of the Weimar government by a fascist regime in Germany in 1933, when almost overnight many long-cherished literary, artistic and liberal views were brought into contempt. Moreover, social-political changes, whether minute and gradual or major and sudden, affect not only morals or customs of various kinds but culture, too—not only literature, but also the arts, education, scholarship and even science. Moreover, even without political upheavals, changes of style, themes and taste are rarely achieved by mere argument or example; they too presuppose the founding of literary and artistic groups, the aid of patrons or institutions or even the state. In short ethics always affects politics and politics continually interferes with ethics.

For many centuries people, and not least philosophers, have had to fight to safeguard their lives, freedom and property against the power of arbitrary government; and on the whole their struggle has been successful, at least in what is known as the democracies of the West. Nevertheless new influential authorities have grown up in recent times, and it appears that the rights conceded to them are not fully in line with democratic principles and thought. These authorities are publicly supported institutions; the excessive esteem in which they are held is a feature of our time. To understand this recent development we have to revert to a fact noticed before, namely, the admiration, or indeed the cult, of 'personality' engendered and instilled in the minds of many by the philosophers of the nineteenth and the early part of the twentieth centuries. Personality was first endowed with a divine faculty—practical reason—by Kant; then with the sovereignty of the state, albeit within the individual's own limited domain, by J. S. Mill; Kierkegaard gave it the arbitrariness of the Deity, which he conceived as irrational; it was credited with the power of legislation by Nietzsche, and finally with divine creativeness by the 'apostles of culture'—the literary, art and music critics. What this excessive cult of personality—of 'genius', 'charisma'—was to lead to, the history of our own time with its dictatorships and unparalleled persecutions has unhappily shown. Small wonder then that not only did the admiration of personality come to and end after the Second World War but the pendulum swung backwards almost violently. And so it happened that the prestige formerly accorded to personality was not so much abolished as transferred—to establishments, organizations, institutions.

Of course there have always been great institutions, of which the most eminent has been the Church, but a comparison of the old organizations with their modern counterparts reveals some important differences. Although modern institutions are perhaps no less conservative or even dogmatic than were their predecessors from the Middle Ages to the eighteenth century, they also incorporate—surprisingly—some of the features arising from the romantic conception of personality. For instead of being merely tradition-bound, they are also time-bound and sometimes consciously and deliberately so, and—dare I say it?—caprice-bound. Frankly arbitrary in the exercise of their authority, they often proclaim and stubbornly cling to paradoxical views such as no individual would venture to express or be able to maintain. This state of affairs unfortunately has also led to the intrusion of politics into fields which used to be free of all political influence, from sport to the Nobel prize, and even to a certain curtailment of free speech, less by repressive action than by a refusal to discuss views which have not been nurtured within an organization's own restricted circles but have emerged from outside. We should therefore try to change Opinion on this aspect of present-day life, first by arguing and pleading, and then, if pleading, however eloquent, does not suffice, by calling for official action or government intervention. Such intervention could be aimed at one of two alternatives: ensuring that no single authority enjoys a monopoly but that on the contrary there is competition between organizations devoted to the same objective—say, the furtherance of literature—or combating the influence of institutions as such by offering patronage to individuals directly. In this way, even though some open censorship may continue to be exercised, governments would make it easier for writers and artists to escape censorship in its more hidden forms.

F. Politics

The problem of designing an ideal form of government has never been solved, and indeed it is difficult to conceive of any possible solution. At the root of the problem is an inescapable dilemma: there cannot exist a government which is able to rule without the vigorous and devoted support of a particular section, or sections, of the community; but no government which has to minister to special interests can possibly be fair or just to the community as a whole. This then is the basic position: it is impossible for any kind of government to be just to *all*, because every government depends on some particular minority group or groups—the army, the aristocracy, the landowners, the industrialists, the financiers, the guilds or the trade unions, in order to govern.

When this is understood, the question will naturally be asked: Which kind of government is the best in this world of ours? Clearly the answer is: that government which is closest to the ideal status of complete independence from any special group interest. Surprisingly monarchy—at least in theory—in the form of 'enlightened absolutism' comes nearest to the ideal condition. For the kings and queens of the sixteenth, seventeenth and eighteenth centuries stood so far above their subjects, whether these were noble or lowly, rich or poor, that they were in fact independent, at any rate to a higher degree than other rulers, of power groups within the nation—though not of course of their own chosen advisers or favourites. Moreover the monarch's right to his throne was unchallengeable. A legitimate monarch could have no rival, and neither domestic intrigues nor defeats in foreign wars could deprive him of his claim to the throne, which rested on inviolate legitimacy.

Still, the era of enlightened absolutism did not last. The monarchs allowed the nobility, which had been subdued, to rise again and so once more became dependent on a privileged class.

In our time democracy is regarded as the only acceptable, legitimate, form of government. The right of democratic governments to rule rests on the doctrine of the sovereignty of the people, which elects them. However, this means of course, in practical terms, that citizens have to choose between two or more parties or their candidates who aspire to represent them in parliament.[1] But parties have to be organized and, whether or not in office they need a firm basis of support. Democratic governments, it is true, are supported by substantially larger sections of the community than other forms of government were or are—monarchy in its late phases, military dictatorships and so on. Nevertheless they depend on sectional interests and are subject to various kinds of pressure.

A country is probably best served, especially with a two-party system existing in it, if one of the parties is the dominant, the 'national', party while the other acts mainly as a spur to keep the principal party vigorously active, alert and ready to exercise self-criticism, that is to say, if the second party succeeds in becoming the government at rare intervals only, which will prevent too long and uninterrupted a rule by one party, a circumstance which, as experience shows, is apt to lead to abuses of power and other grave failings.[1] For when the second party seriously rivals the first and there are alternating governments in quick succession and at short intervals this may well be considered a sign of a profound crisis, for better or for worse. And it may be foreseen that a new structure of government and society will finally emerge from such a crisis, either by way of a steady and gradual evolution or by a sudden turn of events and violent action.

One more aspect of politics is to be discussed: the relation of governments of different countries with one another. Comparisons between the individual and the state have often been attempted, first by Plato (in the *Republic*), for in many respects the individual

---

[1] F. A. Hayek, *Law, Legislation and Liberty*, vol. 3, London 1979, offers a detailed critical exposition of parliamentary democracy, under which, as he says, the elected representatives of a plurality of a nation wrongly and without moral justification exercise unlimited power (are 'omnipotent') while yet nearly always serving special interests, sometimes of a petty nature. He adds that as a result many people regrettably have lost faith in democracy (pp. 1–17; 134–49). (Sometimes, however, it appears that H.'s main intention is to deprive of unlimited power not so much government in general as parliaments with socialist majorities).

[2] See Aristotle's *Eudemian Ethics* I, 5, on political corruption.

can be described as an 'ideal state', because at least in the face of danger from outside a healthy person is completely united within himself. Besides, he enjoys a large measure of freedom both in speech and action. Still, his freedom is greatly exceeded by that of the state which, on the basis of the concept of sovereignty, claims to be free of *all* limiting rules. On the other hand, the state bears a much wider responsibility than any individual, who only has to care for himself, his family and perhaps his friends, but not for anyone beyond his own immediate circle, at least not in the full sense of the word. Of course he can form opinions on matters affecting the entire community or even mankind; he can make his opinions heard—though not necessarily listened to. But governments are expected to act. They are charged with ensuring the safety or even the well-being of a large number of people. From this difference between the state and the individual an important inference has to be drawn: governments cannot be required to look beyond their proper objective, the safety of their own citizens, and hence there can be only one motive for their actions, namely, selfishness, in the broader sense of national selfishness. It follows that, in contrast to a private person's nature and disposition, *benevolence* towards other states (though not necessarily to a small number of helpless or unfortunate citizens of a foreign country) can play no part in a national government's decisions. Indeed the doctrine of sovereignty positively rules out benevolence towards inhabitants of other countries since it prohibits interference by one sovereign state in the affairs of another.

Although it has thus become clear that the principle of pure selfishness applies to state actions, nevertheless—and this is equally important and should be heeded—even conduct entirely dictated by selfish motives is subject to rules, as Hobbes and Grotius have shown. The relevant rules are those which link self-interest to mutual interest. In other words, if a government wants another government to act in good faith towards it, it must itself act in good faith. Or, unless government *A* fulfils its treaty obligations towards government *B* it cannot expect *any* foreign government to treat with it. Therefore if a state as a matter of policy disregards the treaties it has concluded, that state will probably sooner or later find itself confronted with a coalition of other states against it. Indeed there appears to be more natural justice in international relations than in the dealings of private citizens with one another. An inconsiderate person may well flourish throughout his life as long as his actions, however ruthless, are not seen to be violating the laws of his country, but a state which persistently injures its neighbours and more specifically breaks its solemn agreements may see its territory partitioned, or its influence and power curtailed.

Index